SNOW AND LIQUORICE ALLSORTS

Snow and Liquorice Allsorts is a true account of Jennifer Jones's life between leaving Essex in 1968 at the age of twenty and her arrival in Wales at the end of 1976. Her journey began with a short stay in a haunted house; then for a time she lived, worked and partied in London. Then one day she and her friend Katy agreed they needed a change of scene. They made a decision with a map and a pin, and so began many wonderful years by the coast in North Devon.

Jennifer's life took another abrupt turning when she accepted a dare to become a crew member of a yacht. It was a magical experience, but the skipper missed the tide one day, and now Jennifer lives in the Welsh Valleys with her husband. She spends her days baking and gardening, knits for charity and writes a column for her local newspaper.

SNOW AND LIQUORICE ALLSORTS

Jennifer Jones

ARTHUR H. STOCKWELL LTD
Torrs Park, Ilfracombe, Devon, EX34 8BA
Established 1898
www.ahstockwell.co.uk

British Library Cataloguing-in-Publication Data.
A catalogue record for this book is available
from the British Library.

Arthur H. Stockwell Ltd bears no responsibility
for the accuracy of information recorded in this book.

ISBN 978-0-7223-4354-8
Printed in Great Britain by
Arthur H. Stockwell Ltd
Torrs Park   Ilfracombe
Devon EX34 8BA

CHAPTER ONE

It was my late father who started it all, insisting I was having some sort of breakdown. It was actually more of a lingering depression after one final fight with a boyfriend with whom I had had a long-lasting and very volatile relationship. We had been dating for around two years; I remember watching England win the World Cup in 1966, so it must have been 1968. He had recently lost his brother through a very tragic accident. The young man (he was only twenty-three years old) was travelling home on the train late at night after spending the evening drinking with friends. The train slowed and he leant out of the window to see what was happening. His skull was crushed by the tunnel the train had entered. He was alone in the carriage and wasn't discovered until the train pulled into the next station. The boyfriend had to make all the arrangements as his parents were too distraught to do anything and were both on medication from their doctor.

We had to go and view the body at the chapel of rest. I had never seen anyone dead before and although the funeral people had done their best they couldn't disguise the fact that the back of his head was missing. It affected us both badly, but instead of drawing us closer put a wedge between us and he was so angry, both with the circumstances of his brother's death and his lack of ability to cope with the aftermath and comfort his grieving parents.

I think my mother and father were fed up with me moping

about the house and could do or say nothing to help me. They decided that a holiday somewhere would ease my pain, so all the various relatives on the north coast of England, where my father was born, were contacted to see where I would be made the most welcome and cosseted.

The following week I found myself speeding northwards. I was met at the station by a round, twinkly lady with rosy cheeks and button eyes dressed in extremely sensible tweedy clothes despite the unusually warm spring weather – it was early March. She engulfed me in her arms and swept me outside into her battered old car and we were off. She introduced herself as Daisy, my second cousin, and wasn't it wonderful she had me for two whole weeks! She had three children to keep her busy, but was glad of the opportunity to get to know me better, having last seen me when I was a babe in arms. Her husband was some sort of surgical wizard and was away a lot of the time.

It was a short journey and we approached the house through an impressive pair of black wrought-iron gates. The house was one of eight, standing in a curving crescent fronted by a long sweep of private road overlooking neat gardens which were the size of a small park! Beyond the immaculate lawns and flower beds, bright with nodding daffodils and crocuses, the ground sloped gently away to the cliffs overlooking the sea: grey, brooding and angry as only the North Sea can be.

I have very little memory of most of the house although I do remember the many windows blankly gazing out over the sea. The ceilings and doorways remain in my mind vividly, with delicately carved angels and cherubs – quite breathtaking. The ballroom was also quite splendid, an ocean of the palest-blue flooring. It must have been floorboards, but waxed to an incredible shine. The room also had crystal chandeliers, one hung at each end. They sparkled in the late afternoon sun that flooded through the huge windows, curtained in the palest hues to match the floor and open slightly to admit the sea air.

We ate a huge meal from extremely old exquisitely patterned china, accompanied by the children (three delightful girls between the ages of five and nine with the look of their mother), in a

6

formal dining room with a table which could have seated ten or twelve with ease. Daisy and I washed our meal down with fine wine brought from the cellar that ran underneath the house, while the children, once excused from the table, ran off to their latest game.

Daisy was a very homely lady with many hobbies; how she found the time with that huge house and three lively children amazed me. There was a large garden behind the house and she grew a grand assortment of vegetables. She played the piano, embroidered, knitted, sewed, loved jigsaw puzzles and had two energetic dogs, which she walked for a mile or so every day. She insisted we played duets together and, although she was far more accomplished than I, we passed an enjoyable evening.

I was then shown the guest suite: it must have been thirty feet square. There was a huge double bed with a deep turquoise coverlet and many plump cushions placed against the ornate headboard. The floors were bare apart from exquisite rugs, and highly polished to a warm toffee brown. The rest of the furniture was gleaming mahogany. The curtains, the same deep colour as the bedding, hung down from the ceiling to meet and reflect in the wood below. What impressed me most about that beautiful room, however, were the lights. One hung at each end of the vast room: palest blue inverted glass tulips. I was delighted with it all and put away my belongings. After a leisurely bath in a well-appointed en suite bathroom, which led off the bedroom, I dried myself on fluffy towels left there for me and climbed into that bed.

Then it began: a seeping cold, not unlike a draught through a door that had been left open to admit the night air. Colder and colder it became – an icy chill. At first I wondered if the windows had been left open, but they were closed and it was a warm night. Then I noticed the silence and felt myself struggling to breathe, trembling now with the cold and a sudden inexplicable fear. Suddenly one of those elegant lights flickered and died. The other one was still burning brightly, but it too soon died and I found myself in darkness. It felt as if I was sinking into an endless deep abyss and I was by this time terrified. I lay there trying to think, trying to stay calm, and then those sounds broke the silence – at first just a faint whispering as in wind rustling amongst leaves, but it grew louder and faster. Then I heard singing and laughter which grew closer and closer in that awful blackness. I felt a heaviness on me, then nothing.

I remember no more until I woke. I dressed and hurried downstairs.

"Good God, lass!" gasped Daisy. "You look so pale. Are you unwell?"

Trembling and upset I told her of the experience I had the previous night.

Of course I was waiting for an embrace and an explanation, but she just smiled and reached for my hand. "Och, you being your father's daughter, we didn't think you would be afraid of a few wee ghosties!"

I was due to stay with Daisy and her lovely family for a fortnight. The days were wonderful, walking by the sea with her, the dogs running ahead, salty wind pulling at our clothes and hair, shouting to be heard over the crash of the waves. The nights were an ordeal – still the laughing and whispering, sometimes bangs and scuffles; the cold, which settled around me; an uncomfortable blanket of fear and the unknown. I remained in that beautiful, frightening house for almost a week, but after six nights of broken sleep I left after breakfast the next morning and fled back to London.

My father was really angry and shouted that I should return immediately and what did I think I was made of! I described what I had felt, but he was unmoved. To him it was all so normal, having had many such experiences himself on his visits back to his place of birth. We had a massive row, so I made up my mind that was it – I was leaving home and finding a flat. It was only weeks away from my twenty-first birthday, but as I knew the mood my parents were in there wasn't likely to be much celebrating going on. Nothing would persuade me to return to that house.

Over the following weeks the atmosphere at home became more and more strained. My father had written and apologised to Daisy for my abrupt departure, but he was still extremely annoyed with my behaviour.

CHAPTER TWO

I was working in London at the time in a chemist round the back of a well-known London street towards the West End. We had many famous faces who shopped there, but we grew accustomed to it. When someone from stage or screen came wandering into the store they were treated with the same courtesy as any other customer. Even the rich and famous clean their teeth and wipe their bottoms! It did, however, make the job far more interesting and a lot of name-dropping went on when I had time for a social life. The shop was open twenty-four hours a day, so we often had to work all night.

Having just had two weeks' leave of absence to visit the north and that dreadful but charming house, I had just over a week remaining; I decided I would spend it searching for somewhere to live. I viewed quite a number of flats and bedsitters, but I realised that living alone was not going to be a good idea financially. If I lived close to my place of work, the fares would be cheap but the rent extortionate. If I lived closer to my parents, the fares would be expensive but the rent cheaper. I settled for the latter and started searching. I found one possibility in Leytonstone. (Ever heard of David Beckham? I think he hails from that neck of the woods, and, funnily enough, so did my ex-boyfriend!) The building seemed reasonable from the outside and the empty flat was on the top floor. (Years later my sister remarked that most of the places I lived in were up enormous amounts of stairs!) I stepped into the hallway and the smell hit me: a mixture of stale cabbage and disinfectant. Goodness knows where it was coming from, but the higher I climbed the more pungent it became. The flat itself was reasonably furnished, clean and bright, but I really couldn't envisage myself living with that smell day after day.

I also found, through a mutual friend, a girl who had argued with her parents (it sounded familiar) and was looking for a new home, so I arranged to meet up with her. She was tiny – only around four feet eight inches tall, and pencil-thin. She settled herself in the café, ordered a glass of water (unusual in those days) and proceeded to tell me about her diet and all the foods she couldn't eat and couldn't have anywhere near her; all the allergies she had and how she had to soak her hair in hot olive oil nightly and go to bed with her head wrapped in a hot towel. Why? I didn't ask, but thought it was all a bit of a trial, so we said our farewells.

I telephoned a few 'flat shares', from numbers on cards in shop windows and from local newspapers, but most of them had been taken and the rest just didn't feel right; so I temporarily gave up and decided to try again in a couple of weeks. I was due back to work anyway and wouldn't have time to trawl around.

Now I was free and single again I could start seeing more of my friends. I hadn't been in touch with some of them for quite a while as my boyfriend (now ex-boyfriend) had been somewhat possessive and didn't like the idea of me out with most of them.

My best friend was Katy. She was wonderful and I adored her. She was everything I wanted to be, but wasn't, and never would be. She had long, curly, auburn hair that tumbled round her shoulders, enormous green eyes, eyelashes like windscreen wipers and a figure every man she met drooled over. She was the most amazing person – generous, thoughtful, great fun to be with – and we went everywhere together. She was always full of life and would appear in the shop and drag me off to the latest 'in place' and get me into all sorts of trouble.

One day she rushed into the chemist with her usual enthusiasm and informed me she had someone she wanted me to meet from her home town down on the Sussex coast and, as she was so terribly busy with her latest man, could I look after him until he settled in and found somewhere to live. She fidgeted round the shop and generally drove everyone to distraction until my boss, in exasperation, told me to take the rest of the day off.

Katy dragged me out of the chemist and away past the shops and through the traffic until we were clattering down to the Underground en route to Victoria Station, where she had arranged to meet this mysterious person under the clock at six that evening.

We arrived with minutes to spare and he was already there, standing patiently exactly where Katy had instructed him to be, looking rather lost and vulnerable. His name was James. He was very pale and very blonde and very thin, and for some reason – which, unfortunately, I found out much later was probably maternal – I quite liked him. He had already rented an apartment which he hadn't even seen, so we said our goodbyes to Katy, who was dancing round with impatience, and set off to find his new home.

The apartment he had rented turned out to be a small room, or, more precisely, a large cupboard in a block of identical cupboards in North London. I didn't have anything I particularly wanted to do, so sat and watched while he unpacked his belongings. It didn't take long as he only had a small bag and a rucksack. The room was reasonably furnished with a single bed, a wardrobe and a small cupboard. The kitchen was along the hallway. It wasn't very hygienic and it was poorly equipped, so we decided to head off and find somewhere cheap to eat – or I did and James just followed me. He was really rather sweet – quite gentlemanly and sort of obedient. I felt if I asked him to sit up and beg or lie down and roll over, he would have done so.

When we had eaten he returned to his cupboard and I was back on the Underground again.

Over the following weeks whenever we had any spare time we would go for meals or just sit in his room and talk. Sometimes when I just couldn't face the journey home I would stay with him. Soon we were spending most of our time together. I was

11

just out of a relationship and he was lonely, and after a couple of weeks I was staying with him more and more. I was still living at home on the outskirts of East London and, although it was convenient and I had all my meals provided and my clothes washed, it definitely wasn't very exciting. By this time my parents were hardly speaking to me. We couldn't go on as we were in James's cupboard, though. It was cramped for one, but with two of us it was impossible and it was frustrating being smuggled in and out. (His landlady didn't approve of visitors. She would stand in the hallway, always dressed in a scruffy apron and threadbare slippers with a headscarf covering rollers I never saw her without, arms folded with a disapproving look. And she would sniff!) I wasn't very good at it and always had the irresistible urge to giggle, and James used to get quite cross. The angrier he became the more I wanted to laugh.

We badly needed more space, so decided to look around for a place we could rent together. I found out much later that his landlady had asked him to leave as he was very behind with the rent, so for him the situation was perfect. He set off to hunt for something suitable, while I went home to tell my parents I was leaving and moving in with a friend. Had they known it was a male friend they would have been horrified, but they didn't delve too deeply and helped me pack.

I took the bare essentials on that first trip and returned to meet James to see if he had found anything. He was waiting for me in his cupboard, waving a set of keys triumphantly. He had spent many hours trudging around, but all the flats he had seen were so expensive he had to go further afield than either of us really wanted. I don't think he was very keen to give me the address as it was situated between Wormwood Scrubs and Holloway Prison – ideal if either of us wanted to seriously misbehave! I'm sure we never had anything to worry about – the walls were very high and they were both far enough away not to be a problem. I would have liked to see the flat first, but James had paid rent in advance. It didn't occur to me to ask him where the money had come from; I was so excited about moving into my own flat – well, half a flat – that I got completely carried away. I rushed back home and my parents seemed quite delighted I was going. They asked no questions and there was an awkward moment as I trudged to the end of the garden path and turned to look at them both. They both just half smiled and raised a hand in farewell.

I caught a bus to the station as I had two cases and a couple of bags, made my way to the platform and waited for the next train. I sat on the Underground with my belongings around me, my smiling face reflected in the grimy windows as we paused at stations and hurtled through tunnels, until at last I was back at the cupboard. We bundled James's clothes into his bag and rucksack and headed down his stairs for the last time. We took the Underground again, then dragged our belongings down the road. It wasn't far, thank goodness. The area seemed reasonably pleasant: tree-lined roads, clean pavements and, at that time of day, quiet enough.

When I saw the flat itself it was rather a shock. It smelt very musty – damp and unloved. We opened all the windows – very carefully, as some of them were hanging by rusty screws, and not many of those. Every window had rusty bars across it because the flat was underneath a large house. The kitchen and bathroom were huge, the lounge and bedroom rather smaller and the whole flat decorated in a rather shabby, old-fashioned way. It was cheap, though, and near the station and a few shops, so we settled in together.

It was not exactly domestic bliss, but I had nobody to answer to and could do as I liked. It was cold and damp, as basements sometimes are. Every morning the slugs and snails which had crawled into the kitchen cupboards overnight were evicted. We also had to ensure none had taken shelter in the laundry basket before the contents were taken off to the local launderette. It was the spring of 1969. Money was very tight and sometimes I had to decide whether or not to walk to work, or whether to buy cigarettes or buy food. We were reasonably happy together, and the weeks passed quickly.

One event I remember quite clearly that summer of '69 was a concert by the Rolling Stones in Hyde Park. In those days concerts were free, unlike now. It was the first open-air concert I had been to – an extremely poignant event as the gorgeous Brian Jones had tragically lost his life only a few days previously. There was a heady mix of humanity, the smell of marijuana hung in the air and the atmosphere was electric. Apart from the band themselves there were drummers, their dark skin glistening in the heat from the summer sun. They wore brightly coloured robes and some were dressed in capes of metallic silver feathers. At some point in the show many white butterflies were released to mark Brian's passing. It occurred to me much later these were possibly cabbage whites whose caterpillars would have decimated the nearby gardens and turned healthy brassicas into lace doilies almost overnight!

Summer passed us by, then autumn, when the days grew shorter and there was a chill in the air. The leaves turned golden on the trees, then dried and fluttered to the ground. James went out and bought a paraffin stove, which was extremely smelly, but the only heating we had. The most vivid memory during the following months was being wrapped in blankets huddled round that stove listening to 'Days of Future Past' by the Moody Blues over and over because it was all we had, apart from the radio cassette player we listened to it on. We had the radio on sometimes, but we certainly didn't have a television. Thirty years later I was bought the same album as a Christmas gift and the years fell away. There were days of hunger and never being warm, but the laughter and lack of any responsibility somehow made it seem so wonderful. My wages didn't go very far. I had by now given up my job in the chemist because I just couldn't afford the train fare. I was temping around London then, which was better, as I could pick and choose what I wanted to do and there was plenty of work around. James's work was rather hit-and-miss: he was a caddy for a very famous actor (whom incidentally I had sold a toothbrush to) and loved his job. He would often come home and tell me he had parked the Rolls-Royce for him or he had met some other equally famous celebrities. All our money went on rent, food, cigarettes and the occasional illegal treat. Cheap scraps of meat from the local butcher, discarded scrappy vegetables from the greengrocer's and out-of-date bread from the corner shop were what we mostly survived on. I can't remember having more than one meal a day.

Because of the work James did, he loved acting, and soon discovered a theatre just down the road from where we lived. The building was very elegant and old with a tall, imposing clock tower. It was rumoured to be haunted, which made me feel very apprehensive, but I spent huge amounts of time in the evenings there and never felt afraid. The girls in the company certainly were and wouldn't go to certain parts of the building, especially the tower. Some of the boys were nervous as well, but they would never have admitted to it! The company put on mostly Shakespeare plays, and although I loathed them at school they came to life on the stage and I started to really enjoy sitting by the 'prompt' girl and helping out, which took enormous amounts of concentration. We all took what little food we had and shared everything. It was 'ducky' and 'lovey' and 'darling' all the time.

On the last night of a run it was the props department's responsibility to dream up a trick to play on the cast to see if we could crack them up or not. In one particular play there was supposed to be a mouse in a box, but it was really just a piece of fur. On the last night of that particular run one of the cast brought in their pet rat and popped it into the box instead of the fur. I don't know who was the most surprised, the rat or the actress. The poor girl's screams were very realistic that night!

Occasionally I would sit in the auditorium and watch rehearsals. James was a fine actor and I was very proud of him. On the last night the whole company would stay in the theatre, pull down the old set and put up the new one ready for the next run. It involved mostly carpentry and painting, and the whole company took part. We slept where we fell, draped across seats or sprawled on the floor.

Life went on like that for quite a while and although I wasn't completely happy I was content and busy. I had found out by now that James had a weakness for gambling, which is where he found the money for the advance in our rent! He found it harder and harder to stay away from the bookmakers, and we fought about it endlessly. But things were about to change.

Katy had been popping in with greater frequency. She had moved back to be with her mother on the Sussex coast. Her stepfather had recently passed away following a massive heart attack and Katy had only wanted to stay long enough to sort out his personal effects and ensure her mother had adjusted to the situation well enough to live alone. She then announced she was moving back to London and would stay with us temporarily until she decided what she wanted to do. I was overjoyed to have her there, but she muttered about being in the way and said it wouldn't be for long. She was helping with the rent and had befriended the local butcher, so life improved dramatically. She could wrap any man around her little finger with a toss of that hair, a glance from those eyes and a flutter of eyelashes. She was soon coming home with vast bags of sausages and occasionally some steak or other delicious morsels. We must have lived for months on mostly sausages – this is probably why I'm not that keen on sausages now! We were still very short of money, but at least we had food in our stomachs to keep out the bitter cold.

It must have been just before Christmas when Katy moved in with us. She slept in the lounge in an old, tatty sleeping bag on the floor. I crawled out of bed one morning, fully dressed as usual (we wore more clothes to bed than we did during the day; our relationship was definitely not based on passion!) and I walked into the lounge to be greeted by the most amazing sight. There was a mountain in the middle of the room! The mountain must have been disturbed, for suddenly the covering of snow started to move, slowly at first then gathering speed, not unlike a small avalanche. Katy emerged covered in the blanket of snow which had blown in overnight through the gaps around the window and settled gently around her. She was quite unconcerned about it all and sat there in her sleeping bag with the snow sparkling in that wonderful auburn hair, eating her customary breakfast of Liquorice Allsorts! I always had great admiration for her.

Whatever she did was with such style and confidence; she seemed so worldly and mature. It was only many years later, when we met again, that she confessed she felt I was the more worldly of us. Amazing!

One night Katy came home looking flushed and excited. She had met another man. She then proceeded to tell me how wonderful he was, how charming, how handsome, how rich! Such a man was unheard of in our circle of friends, who were mostly out-of-work actors from the theatre. His name was Tony. She had met him in Chelsea at a party she had somehow been invited to the night before. He sounded perfect for her and I was so pleased to see her looking so happy. She hadn't had an easy time separating herself from her ex-husband, whom she had married when very young (and she had discovered very quickly what a mistake she had made). I had met him only briefly a couple of times, but had taken an instant dislike to him. He was attractive enough, but vain and rather stuffy, pompous as well. She was well rid of him as far as I was concerned. Occasionally she would stay with Tony in Chelsea. The visits became more frequent until she came home only for a change of clothes. I missed her dreadfully.

Things between James and me started to fall apart, with the money worries and his constant gambling. It wasn't entirely his fault. I was miserable without Katy and lonely because James was either in the betting shop or at the theatre. He was hoping to become a professional actor by then and spoke of parts in the West End he was hoping to audition for. The actor who was his boss at the golf club south of London had been to see him in a play and thought he was accomplished enough for a part in a film. James of course wanted to move to a better area to further his career and maybe entertain new friends he hoped to make. I didn't want to move with him, so we parted and I went home to my parents. They weren't overjoyed to see me, but grudgingly said I could stay until I found somewhere else to live.

I gave up temping as the fares had just become too expensive. So I had no job and really nowhere to live. I eventually found a position in the local paint factory, which was a short bus ride away. It smelt awful, but after a while it wasn't so noticeable. I had an extremely small office with just a desk and a chair, a half-dead plant and a tiny window overlooking the car park. My role was to calculate on a slide rule the various amounts of all the chemicals that make up paint. One of the technicians would make up a sample and, if they were happy with it, pass it to me. It was actually quite interesting. The man I worked with, Daniel, was very attractive, but one of those whose wife doesn't understand him. He used to follow me around all the time, trying to get me alone. He was very sweet and it was all rather flattering, but, raw from the relationship with James, I was still wary and I didn't want to start an affair with a married man that would only end in tears. He got the message after a while and physically left me alone. He then proceeded to send me poetry written in bold black on thick cream notepaper – huge envelopes of the stuff! Some of it was gorgeous, but it was mostly very dark and dramatic.

I jogged along like that for a few weeks, but felt rather suffocated back at my parents. It was still winter and very cold. In the mornings the fields around the factory were white with early morning frost and the buses unreliable. The job was enjoyable and I was eating properly again, had clean clothes, was warm and had sheets on the bed, but it was very much the lull before the storm.

I arrived home one day to find Katy on the doorstep; we fell into each other's arms, laughing and crying. My parents were very wary – they knew Katy from our first day together in technical college and if I ever got into trouble it was always Katy cheering me on. They were quite relieved when she said she wasn't staying and cheered up immensely when she said she had a proposition that would get me away from the family home once more.

CHAPTER THREE

Katy wanted us to get a flat together, near enough to Tony so she could see him frequently, but far enough away to give him the space he needed. He hadn't lived with anyone for years, having lost both his parents in a car accident at a very early age. He was then sent off to boarding school by an elderly aunt, who was a spinster and couldn't cope with the upbringing of two young and unruly boys. He was thoroughly miserable there, having no privacy and no time to himself at all. His parents had left both him and his brother (whom we met and got to know a lot later) extremely well off and, thanks to the family solicitor, who had invested wisely, he hadn't really needed to work. Katy thought she would stand more of a chance of keeping the relationship afloat by keeping her distance, so we spent an enjoyable evening circling all the flat ads in the paper and generally being very dramatic and silly! My mother peered round the door occasionally and once arrived with tea and biscuits for us both – more out of curiosity than goodwill, I'm sure. The paper resembled a huge game of noughts and crosses by the time we had finished. Most of them – in fact, nearly all of them – were completely out of our reach financially, and as Katy wanted to live in West London we decided we would have to share with one or two other people if we wanted somewhere desirable to live.

One option that seemed reasonable, however, was a houseboat in Chelsea which we could possibly manage without starvation.

It appealed to both of us and was near Tony. Katy rushed off to ask his opinion and arranged for him to go and see it, as we didn't really know London that well at the time and the address meant nothing to us. He arranged to view it and discovered it was a stone's throw from his Chelsea house. Unfortunately it was almost derelict and it would have cost a great deal to make it habitable. It was very small and dark, and after much poking around he discovered rather a serious leak under the floor. Of course it could have been a possibility, but I feel he thought being on the river could be dangerous. Neither of us could swim, and I think he had visions of us coming home one dark night, drunk or stoned, tripping over and ending up in the Thames, or indeed the same fate occurring to him and any visitors we might have in the future. He didn't even consider taking us down there in case we fell in love with it.

The next best thing we found was an attic flat very near Portobello Road – a part of London we both agreed would be ideal for us. Katy decided she would ring that evening if it wasn't too late when she got back to Tony's. I woke the next morning to the insistent ringing of the doorbell, crawled out of bed and went downstairs to open the front door, and there was Katy leaning on the bell push looking like she had been awake for hours – which apparently she had! It was only seven o'clock and my mother was not at all amused. My father, however, saw the funny side of it and wandered off to shut himself in the kitchen with his breakfast and newspaper. Katy told me she had rung the number in the paper and had arranged to view the flat that morning.

After a quick wash I threw on some clothes, made sure I looked reasonably tidy and we were on our way. The journey seemed very slow, although it was only about twenty or so stops on the Underground, but journeys seem endless when the destination holds such excitement. We jumped off the train at the appropriate stop and the escalator carried us up to street level. Katy had been given directions and the station was actually on the corner of the street where the house was situated.

At last we were standing outside the property. It looked absolutely stunning and we grinned at each other in delight. It was huge and white-walled. We could see what appeared to be a large garden full of trees, accessible by a tiny winding path through a stone archway and disappearing round the back of the house. The front door was half-panelled with tiny panes of stained glass, and to the right of the doorway was a bank of bell pushes. We amused ourselves for a while reading all the names and trying to imagine who they were, then rang the bell at the top which simply said 'penthouse'. Very grand!

We stood there for what seemed a very long time until at last the front door was opened by a very slim, pretty girl with waist-length, almost black hair, smooth coffee-coloured skin, big, dark eyes and a welcoming smile. She introduced herself as Lea and led us into the house and up the stairs. On and on we climbed until we reached a door about a foot from the floor. Katy and I looked at each other with amusement and I know we were thinking the same thing: *Alice in Wonderland*! Lea opened the door to reveal a small staircase enclosed by yellow-painted walls and a yellow ceiling. The stair carpet was also bright yellow and it gave the illusion of passing through a strange yellow tunnel. Katy and I were quite out of breath when we reached the top.

Lea bustled off to put the kettle on and left us to recover and look round. The hallway was almost square with four doors leading from it which all stood open so we could see into each room. The bathroom was to the left, at the rear of the house. It was painted black and silver apart from the inside of the bath, washbasin and toilet pan. The black tiles on the floor were sprayed here and there with silver moons and stars. The windows were also black, with the same moon and stars etched upon them. The kitchen, which was directly opposite the bathroom, overlooking the street, was a bright pillar-box red – the fridge, cooker, plates, floor, ceiling . . . everything. During the following months I found I could cook a meal, serve it, wash up and put everything away without moving at all; that's how small that kitchen was, but it was delightful. The lounge was absolutely magnificent: gold and green with plants everywhere, gigantic, soft, plump cushions and rugs scattered around on the pale bare floorboards. There was no furniture at all. As we stood there on that spring day (by now it was 1970) the sun was bright and, with the breeze gently ruffling the gold draped curtains, the room almost seemed to shimmer. The bedroom was to the rear of the house, overlooking the garden. It was decorated in every colour of the rainbow, but instead of looking chaotic it just seemed perfect in every way. It was the largest room and there were three beds and three wardrobes.

We gratefully accepted the tea Lea had made for us and made ourselves comfortable in the sunlit room. Lea was charming. She was actually Australian, but her accent was soft and appealing. She'd had two fellow Australians living there until the previous week, but they had left to return to their native land so she needed to replace them quickly. Lea explained she had seen quite a few people, but they either didn't like the flat (how could they not!) or she didn't like them. She told us some great tales of the stories some of the prospective flatmates had told her – a great mimic, she soon had us crying with laughter. She thought that as Katy and I obviously knew each other well we only had to get to know her and vice versa. Soon we were discussing rent and bills and working out equal shares of it all.

We left her then, having assured her we would return the next day with our belongings. We made our way back down that magical staircase and on down the stairs into the street. We hugged each other joyfully. We had both fallen in love with the flat, and Lea seemed really sweet. We rushed back to the station, found a phone box and rang Tony to tell him the news. He was delighted; and as it was a Saturday the following day (when we planned to move in) he suggested taking us both out to lunch on the Sunday to celebrate finding our new home. We went our separate ways full of plans and hopes for the future.

We moved into that wonderful house the following day as planned. It was a beautiful morning and the sun was warm on our faces as we carried our belongings up the yellow staircase.

We didn't have that much. The flat was furnished, so it was just clothes and personal items. It did, however, take most of the day as we had to make several journeys on the Underground both from my parents' house and from Tony's, where Katy had left most of her possessions. It was early evening before it was all in and we could stop for a break before we put it all away. Lea produced a bottle of wine she had found in the back of one of the wardrobes – hidden and forgotten by one of the previous tenants, I presume. Katy and I had brought a bottle as well, so we had three bottles of wine to drink. Lea made a wonderful curry for us. She could make amazing dishes out of the most meagre ingredients, which was a revelation for both of us. (Katy could hardly boil an egg, but Lea patiently taught us over the weeks and months how to rustle up nutritious and filling meals with speed and little financial outlay.) After clearing away and tidying the tiny kitchen we settled down for the evening.

Lea wanted to show us the garden, so down all those stairs once again we went, out through the front door and round the pathway under the archway. The garden lay before us, quiet and secretive. All the tenants had keys. We were soon sitting on a rustic bench beneath the rustling trees. It was so peaceful that it was hard to imagine we were in the West End of London; the traffic was just a distant hum. We had taken our glasses and the remainder of the wine with us, and we solemnly touched glasses to one another's future then sat quietly together, each wondering which direction our lives would now take. Eventually, as the air cooled, we left that secret place, locked the gate carefully behind us and went back inside and up the stairs once more. We spent the next few hours packing away the remainder of our belongings and making up beds before wishing each other goodnight.

We slept extremely well after all that exercise, food and wine and woke refreshed and ready to face our new life. We lay there lazily, chatting for a while, then Katy suddenly remembered we were meeting Tony for lunch and it was a great rush to make ourselves presentable. In those days bathing and deciding what to wear took me an incredible amount of time. Hair tied back or left loose? What shoes? What clothes? How much make-up?

At last we were ready. Lea was asked to join us, but she had arranged to meet friends and departed down the stairs with a cheery wave. Little did I know as we set off to meet Tony that my life was about to change dramatically.

CHAPTER FOUR

We had no idea how to get to the restaurant Tony had suggested, so we decided we would splash out and hail a cab. We walked down our street to the main road by the Underground station and quickly waved one down and were soon speeding off. Shortly we arrived at the address Katy had given the driver, climbed out, and found ourselves standing outside a shop which appeared to be a very closed shop! We were quite taken aback and wondered if we had the right address. Then we noticed a very small handwritten sign pinned to the wall pointing to the basement. Down the steps we went and pushed open the door.

We were met with a wall of colour and sound. It seemed at that moment the whole of London was there, packed into the small room crowded with tables and chairs. We stood there agog with our senses reeling. Then a huge hairy figure dressed in what appeared to be a large animal skin, jeans and boots, bawled to us from the corner of the room. The vision arose, came lumbering towards us and enveloped Katy in his huge tree-like arms. This was my first glimpse of Tony. In that tiny space he seemed absolutely enormous and he had such a presence. All I could do was stand and stare. He let go of Katy eventually and turned his gaze upon me. He had such a beautiful face, long, untidy golden hair, a shaggy beard and the gentlest hazel eyes, full of laughter. He put one of his huge arms round my shoulders, propelled me across the room to where he had been sitting and introduced me to the three boys he had been sharing a table with. He had a voice like dark velvet, hypnotic and captivating. No wonder Katy was crazy about him! I felt carried rather than escorted. I was pushed into a chair and had a huge glass of what I presumed was wine thrust into my hand. I sipped it slowly and it was delicious, ice-cold, sweet and fruity. We were mostly wine drinkers in those days – apart from Tony, who drank pints of whisky and orange.

He then began to introduce me to his friends. Sitting next to me was Alan. He seemed the quietest of them all. He was simply dressed in a T-shirt and jeans, quietly spoken, tall and slim with floppy brown hair, brown eyes and a smattering of freckles across the bridge of his nose. Next to him was Chris, who was shouting and telling jokes, waving his arms around and making rather a lot of noise. He was tiny with long blonde hair and big blue eyes and wore a bright-red shirt and yellow check trousers. Every time our paths crossed he was always dressed in bright clothes and was always very loud and very funny. Then I was introduced to Max and my stomach flipped over. He was tall, and wore huge tinted sunglasses, with skin smooth and tanned. Dark, almost black, hair curled crisply against his collar. He was very smartly dressed, with well-pressed trousers and a gorgeous shirt, and he was even wearing a cravat! He had an air about him – not the presence Tony had, but a certain style and confidence that immediately fascinated me. He smiled lazily at me and bent to kiss my hand. I couldn't take my eyes off him as he laughed and joked with the others. They were all teasing Katy as she sat there looking flushed and happy.

The waitress came over and, after a lot of banter and leg-pulling which made the poor girl blush furiously, everyone decided what they wanted to eat and she scuttled off. Katy ordered for both of us as she could see I felt rather out of my depth with all these new people and she knew exactly what I preferred to eat anyway. I cannot recall what I ate, but I know the food was spicy and plentiful.

After what seemed a long time, full of good food and excellent wine we found ourselves back outside, blinking in the bright sunshine. Tony took over then, and I found myself in another cab heading for the boys' house in Chelsea, not far from where Tony was living. I remember feeling slightly panicky and aware of a course of events unfolding that I had no control over, but at the same time I was feeling rather smug that I seemed to have been accepted into their circle. They all seemed very mature, but in fact weren't much older than us. They had all been through the public-school system together in Lincolnshire and there obviously existed a strong bond between them. They had enjoyed their independence for quite a while and were very comfortable with it and one another.

The house they shared in Chelsea was a typical bachelor home, full of unwashed cups and plates, remains of takeaways and unmade beds, although spacious and extremely well furnished. Katy and I washed some cups and made coffee while the boys all settled down with the Sunday papers, bickering with good humour over who was going to read what first. They bought every Sunday paper every week. It was a ritual for them: a long lie-in, a leisurely lunch then home for a good read. Someone put on some music – I can't now recall what it was – and I curled up in a chair to drink my coffee. With the music playing in the background and the murmur of voices if one of them found a juicy titbit he thought the others would find amusing, my eyelids grew heavier and heavier and soon I was asleep. I don't know how long I slept, but I woke with a start and looked around me.

The room at first seemed empty but as I cautiously sat up I saw a figure sprawled on the sofa. He turned to look at me. It was Max! He explained that Tony and Katy had gone to the cinema (there was a film showing they had been waiting to see for weeks) and he had assured Katy he would take care of me and drive me home when I was ready to leave. There was no sign of either Chris or Alan, and I presumed they had also departed. He asked if I would like more coffee and left the room. I had a mirror in my bag and had a quick peek to see if I looked presentable. Apart from looking slightly crumpled, I looked all right, so I just dragged a comb through my hair (which fortunately was long and straight) and sat down again. Max soon returned with a steaming mug, which I accepted gratefully.

All that food and wine had made me very thirsty.

Soon I suggested it was time I left. I didn't want to outstay my welcome and didn't know if Max had any plans. He led me out of the house and there, parked by the kerb, was a sky-blue Morgan sports car. I saw the same car on an advertising hoarding weeks later and discovered Max had been paid a princely sum for allowing it to be photographed. He helped me into the passenger seat and hopped in behind the wheel, and we roared off. I was speechless. I pinched myself to make sure I wasn't dreaming, but this was for real. I was sitting in a beautiful open-topped sports car on a bright summer's day with a gorgeous man. He drove well, but very fast, and all too soon we were home. He helped me out, kissed my hand once more, and then drove away in a cloud of dust, leaving me open-mouthed on the pavement. I had hoped he would ask to see me again, but Max, I was to discover, was like that: he used to drive me totally insane, strolling in and out of my life when it suited him. I couldn't plan anything because I always desperately wanted to see him. I don't think he even realised he was doing it and certainly had no idea what a devastating effect he had on me.

I quietly let myself into the house and made my way upstairs into my home. Katy was still out with Tony and I knew Lea wouldn't be back until later that evening, so I ran a bath and lay down in the soothing water. My senses were still reeling from the events of the day, the people I had met, the house in Chelsea, but especially Max. The water eventually cooled and I dried myself, put on a dressing gown and wandered restlessly from room to room. I couldn't wait to see Katy and see what she knew, if anything, about Max. I found a book and sat down to read, but I couldn't concentrate at all.

At last I heard footsteps coming up the stairs and Katy's smiling face peeped round the door. She was eager to know how I had got along with Max and was full of apologies for going out and leaving me, but said I had looked so peaceful curled up in that chair that it seemed almost cruel to wake me. She couldn't tell me very much about Max at all, only that he originally came from Lincolnshire, like the rest of the boys, owned properties all over London and was considerably well off. She'd had a lovely evening with Tony, and she said putting some distance between them seemed to have brought their initial closeness back. We talked until Lea came home, then we all retired for the night.

We overslept the next morning, much to Katy's dismay. She was furious with herself as she would be late for work and her boss was unbelievably mean. He would stop an hour's pay if she was a minute late. She loved her job, however, which was as a bookmaker's assistant.

When she had washed and dressed, she rushed off down the stairs swearing away to herself. I had a long, leisurely breakfast, dressed reasonably smartly and took myself off for some serious job-hunting, after first ringing the paint factory and telling them I would not be returning. I wanted something a little more challenging than endless filing and typing, so I called at my favourite employment agency to see what they had to offer. There was a lot of work available; employers would almost be falling over themselves to get you off the agencies' books and on to theirs. One vacancy sounded interesting – mostly reception work, a little typing and 'other duties as and when necessary'.

I soon found myself outside a grubby little building in Hatton Garden, cheek by jowl with some very exclusive jewellers. It turned out to be an art and photographic studio and the outside was very deceptive. Through the doors I stepped into another world, all glass and chrome everywhere, very smart. When they discovered I had spent some considerable time in the theatre they asked me if I could start immediately, although to me it didn't seem to have any bearing on the job at all. The switchboard was small and easy to operate, being very similar to one I had operated at a publisher's many years before, so there were no problems there. The typing was mainly compiling timetables, making sure everyone knew when and where they were supposed to be for every hour of every day. It was a lot of fun, and I soon got to know the models that were based there, prancing in through the door with their endless legs, bitchiness and vanity. I soon realised why my theatrical experience had appealed to them. The models went from one crisis (usually imaginary) to another, and most of the actors at that glorious theatre had been very similar. I found the rest of the staff extremely helpful and settled in quickly.

One in particular I hit it off with straight away. His name was Simon, typically scruffy as he was a freelance artist, extremely talented and much sought after, he came and went when he pleased. He was a handsome boy, not much taller than me with a wicked sense of humour and gorgeous blue eyes. He was 'spoken for' as he put it, but I never met his girlfriend, although I spoke to her on the phone frequently. Simon and I used to lunch together whenever we could and found some great cheap little restaurants tucked away down side streets close to the studio. He was fun to be with and helped take my mind off Max, who by then was really getting under my skin.

Life drifted through the spring. I wasn't seeing a great deal of Katy, who was still with Tony, but the relationship didn't seem to be progressing as Katy really wanted. He began to drop by the studio to see me, and as I got to know him better I grew closer to him. Out of his affection for me he began to question my relationship with Max. He said he was concerned as Max had a stream of broken hearts behind him and Tony didn't want mine added to the list. He seemed quite bewildered with his relationship with Katy; as they had become lovers early on they didn't seem to have formed any sort of friendship at all.

Around Easter Lea suddenly announced she was leaving us. She had enjoyed her time in England, but missed her friends and family back home. We would be sorry to see her go, but decided to hold a party for her. It was decided it would be a dressy affair. Katy wore a floor-length halter-necked dress in a beautiful shade of green with silver sandals. She looked absolutely stunning. I wore the brightest-pink dress. It had frills around the shoulders and hem, just skimming my knees. Bright sandals completed the outfit. Katy piled my hair on top of my head in huge coils and used most of a can of hairspray to keep it there. Lea wore gold, which shone and shimmered as she moved gracefully among us. With her milky coffee skin she looked amazing. She had laid out a huge buffet of spicy treats and little cakes. Tony and the boys arrived, and even my lovely sister came, although for some reason she took an instant dislike to Tony. I never found out why, but his appearance was somewhat alarming that night: scruffy boots and jeans and his huge smelly coat! The rest of our guests wore their best clothes. The house was packed. We left every flat and bedsit door open, and as one went up or down the stairs the music changed depending on who was playing what and where. It was a wonderful night, and the party went on until the dawn came up and everyone started to drift away.

We knew we couldn't manage the expense of the flat with just the two of us and so advertised for a third person to join us. When the advertisement appeared in the paper, the phone rang constantly. We took it in turns to answer it. We had a few odd calls. One chap asked if he moved in could he sleep with us both in turn? And he asked what underwear we had! Another had three dogs, two cats and a rabbit. Out of all the calls, we narrowed it down to ten and asked them to come round for a chat. We had a steady stream of people up and down the stairs – mostly girls, but a few boys, which we decided against eventually as there was only one bedroom. After they had all left we sat and thought about it for a long time. As we would be living so closely together, the ability to see eye to eye was essential.

It was difficult to decide who would fit in with us with only half an hour's chat to base it on, but we both fortunately decided on the same person. Her name was Robyn. Her parents were of mixed race and she looked surprisingly like Lea, but had been born in London. She had been very direct and honest with us and was desperate for somewhere to live as she was in a very difficult and violent relationship. She just wanted to walk away – preferably when her partner was not at home, so he didn't know where she was. Apart from needing a home, she enjoyed the same taste in music, read the same books and had a crazy infectious sense of humour, so we rang her and offered her the flat-share. She was thrilled and arrived the next day. Within a week it felt as though she had always been there.

I was spending a lot of time in the house then, afraid to go anywhere in case I missed Max, so I was getting to know the other occupants of the house quite well. On the stairs by our little door that was a foot from the floor were two doors. One led to a bathroom and the other to a lounge with a tiny kitchen (it was actually smaller than ours) and a bedroom. In this flat was a girl called Trixie. She was a wild child! She was blonde and voluptuous and wore extremely low-cut, very short, tight-fitting clothes. She was not the sort of girl to take home for tea with the parents. She lived there alone so must have had an income from somewhere, but I wasn't going to ask! She went out at odd times, ran a car and had a huge wardrobe full of clothes, a beautiful sound system and some great furniture. She was great fun, but totally unpredictable. She rarely wore clothes when she was home, and any strangers in the house had a bit of a shock when she strolled out of her lounge to use the bathroom. She didn't mind at all, and would lean on the wall and chat to whoever was passing by. If anyone actually went into her flat – especially her bedroom – they were in for another shock. Above her bed (which appeared to be a Bedouin tent) she kept a huge leather whip on a hook. I don't know if she actually used it, but she would bring her 'guests' home for 'coffee', and she soon sorted the men from the boys. Most of them couldn't get out of the door fast enough. She hadn't been living there very long. Her brother was a good friend of Alan, and he often came to visit.

On the floor below there were two bedsitters, with a small communal bathroom. In the front of the house was a young boy called Arthur, who came from up north – somewhere around Newcastle, I think, judging by his accent. He was very small and really daft, always dressed from top to toe in leather. He had painted the whole flat purple and black and had glued a pair of biker boots to the ceiling so it appeared someone was about to fall through! He also liked some very strange music, which he used to play all day and most of the night. The only album I ever recognised was Captain Beefheart, but the rest I had never heard before and haven't heard since. He lived mostly on baked beans, cold and straight from the tin. He was always pleasant, though, and ready for a chat. In the back of the house on the same floor lived a young couple, Dave and Sandra. She was small and dark and he was tall and blonde. They wore long flowing robes and didn't own a pair of shoes between them. Music would always be playing. They enjoyed the mournful Leonard Cohen. Joe Cocker and Leon Russell would also be heard frequently. 'Mad Dogs and Englishmen' springs to mind, but they played some great stuff. They lived quietly together, but kept a keen eye on everyone else and never let anyone go hungry. They did the rounds every night, quietly enquiring if all had eaten; if not, they were given a plate of whatever Sandra had cooked that day – usually brown rice with an assortment of vegetables, as they were strictly vegetarian. Arthur ate with them most evenings, and Sandra watched over him constantly.

In the basement was what we thought was an old man. He was probably only around forty years of age, but to us that seemed ancient. His name was Nigel and he just seemed a bit odd. None of us – not even the boys – would go down alone for any reason. He was probably a very lonely man, but would insist on touching everyone in a most intimate way. He had a beautiful home filled with antiques, was always immaculately dressed and adored classical music. He played the flute in an orchestra somewhere and was always lurking on the stairs, trying to get us into his flat to listen to his music or to borrow the wonderful book he had just read or to admire a piece of art. We were all really rather rude to him, but he was very persistent.

I was still spending my days with Simon, my lovely friend from work. It was an easy-going, completely platonic relationship we were both very comfortable with. He was very serious about his girlfriend, and I still had an aching longing for Max to want to spend more time with me. He still turned up from time to time, but we usually just went for a ride in the car or for a walk somewhere, usually on a Sunday morning. Close by was an open-air gallery with some excellent artwork for sale strung up on nearby railings, and many of the artists for a small fee would sketch anyone who was interested. Some of them were very talented and we spent hours watching them. Our relationship was not really satisfactory at all, but at least I saw him. He then suddenly began to come round much more often, never came empty-handed and was extremely generous. He brought exquisitely packed little trinkets, perfect posies and out of season fruit from some exotic place. Sometimes the gifts rendered me speechless. One day he surprised me with a hamper courtesy of one of his wide circle of friends, who worked for a very famous store. (The friend worked in what I presumed was the pet department and at weekends or days off would take home assorted animals and birds to care for. I remember visiting on one occasion and there was a tiny lion cub sprawled on the carpet.) The hamper was packed with sumptuous food: tiny sandwiches and pastries, small, sweet cakes and savoury biscuits with pâtés, cheeses and fruit. Also in the large wicker basket there were small perfumed damp towels, champagne and crystal glasses. He took me to one of the London parks. It was so peaceful lying on the blanket Max had so thoughtfully provided, feeling the summer breeze on our faces. He was very secretive about his life in general, and after a while I ceased to question him. I was willing to accept our relationship on his terms. Life rolled along. I was living in a great house with fantastic people and my job was really enjoyable.

It was a balmy summer evening and I had just climbed out of the bath when Trixie (naked as usual) came rushing breathlessly up the stairs. She reached the top and leant weakly against the wall to get her breath back, then asked if I knew a mysterious-looking man who wore dark glasses and drove a very expensive sports car; and if I did, could I please go downstairs and ask him to stop leaning on the doorbell because it was driving her crazy. Max! I dressed quickly, hoping I looked reasonably tidy, dragged a comb through my hair and rushed downstairs; and there he was, standing on the doorstep with a bottle of wine in one hand and a bouquet of flowers in the other, just presuming I would ask him in – which, of course, I did. I felt very flustered. It was the first time he had been inside the flat; usually he just called

34

for me. He followed me upstairs. Katy and Robyn were out so we had the place to ourselves. I gave him a guided tour, which didn't take very long, and he seemed pleased I was so obviously happy there. I rummaged in the drawers in the kitchen and found a corkscrew, and while he uncorked the wine and made himself comfortable on one of the massive cushions I arranged the flowers and found some glasses. The evening went very quickly. We sat and talked of music, books, food and wine and he was charming company. He looped his arm around my shoulder as we sat together and I found it difficult to concentrate. All I wanted was to curl into him; he smelt divine and looked so handsome.

It was soon time for him to leave and he gave me a chaste peck on the cheek and wandered off down the stairs. I hoped he would return, sweep me off my feet and haul me off to bed, but he didn't and I watched his car pull away from the kerb with mounting frustration. I didn't know whether to be pleased he hadn't seduced me, disappointed he hadn't tried or worried that he just might not be interested. By the time Katy came home I had worked myself into frenzy.

CHAPTER FIVE

The next big event was when the boys in the Chelsea house were told they had to move out as the house was being demolished. They had been living there for quite some time, but their landlord had been offered a considerable sum for the property as the area was about to be redeveloped. So it was time for them to move on.

Alan went back to Lincolnshire with Chris. Tony went to stay with his gorgeous brother, Timothy, who was six feet four inches, and gay. Timothy owned a vast penthouse apartment overlooking the River Thames and lived there with his American Negro boyfriend, who was exactly five feet tall. The penthouse was amazing. The building itself had a uniformed doorman. In the hallway was a reception desk, behind which stood cubbyholes with letters and parcels for the residents. To the left were two rich brown leather sofas where guests could wait until summoned by their hosts; and to the right were two elevators, which would deliver you swiftly and with a quiet hiss to the chosen floor. As the doors opened you were met by a sea of pastel carpet leading on to their home. They had a huge lounge painted pale grey with darker-grey carpet and black rugs and furniture. The kitchen was surprisingly compact, but beautifully fitted. And the bedroom! Everything in it was a shade of pink, from the blinds to the covering on the bed, the flooring and even the ceiling. There were bright ribbons, beads and feathers everywhere, hanging from cupboards, draped over mirrors and climbing two massive vases standing on each side of the windows and filled with twigs, which had also been sprayed a vibrant pink.

Max decided he would move in with me until he found a flat he could buy (all his property was rented out). From what I remember, he presumed I would just love the idea. I had very mixed feelings about the situation, however. The earlier obsession I had felt for him had faded somewhat, and although I was still very fond of him the spark had dimmed. Where once there had been fireworks and elation there was now the occasional sparkler, but I was still happy to be with him. My belongings were moved down from the top of the house to the floor below, so Katy was now with Robyn and Richard (Robyn's brother), who had arrived the week before and was dark and exotic-looking like his sister. I was now sharing with Trixie, and we had Dave, Sandra and daft little Arthur on the floor below. Max had put his furniture into storage, and we bought a sofa bed because, as far as I knew, Max wouldn't be there for very long and we didn't have a lot of room for anything else.

It took quite a few weeks to adjust to living with him. He had his good points, of course. He was extremely domesticated, which surprised me considering the chaotic lifestyle he had shared with the boys in Chelsea, but it was probably just as well as my prowess was in the bedroom, not the kitchen! He was an accomplished cook and conjured up the most amazing meals in that tiny kitchen, washed the dishes and tidied the kitchen when we had eaten our fill. He was a wonderful lover and he taught me so much. I found that men whom I had physical relationships with in the years to come were sadly lacking by comparison. He was a warm, funny, passionate man and completely insatiable! The car came too, of course, which was very convenient for lifts to work, but he drove me to distraction. He was so meticulous in everything he did and so vain about his appearance. He always seemed to be in the bath or generally preening himself in front of the mirror. He liked to look immaculate at all times, not a hair out of place, moustache perfectly trimmed, skin moisturised, clothes freshly pressed and sunglasses polished daily.

We lived together for around six months until he felt he needed something more luxurious to fit in with his image and asked me to go flat-hunting with him. By now things had rather gone into reverse: he had become extremely fond of me, but he had rather fallen off his pedestal. This was probably a good thing as it evened the relationship out a bit. From then we got on well and I didn't mind where he went or whom he saw. I think this rather irritated him.

Timothy (Tony's brother) and his boyfriend then announced that they too were looking for a new home as they had now decided that the penthouse they had been sharing, which to me had seemed perfect, was too small. They were searching for something in the same area, but with at least two bedrooms as Tony had been sleeping on the floor. They wanted to come and stay temporarily with me until they found something they both liked and could afford. So Max moved out and they moved in. It was all rather a squash. I slept on Trixie's floor and wandered off to see Sandra when she had one of her numerous visitors while the boys took over the sofa bed in the other room. They were tremendous fun and one or other of them would settle down on the lid of the toilet for long chats while I bathed. The conversations were mostly about clothes and make-up. Both Tony and Tim had worn eyeshadow for some time, and Tim and his boyfriend adored clothes. They bickered and argued constantly. Timothy was very like his brother, tall and imposing with an almost regal presence about him. I felt sometimes it was all rather a waste as girls would fall over themselves to be introduced and were always very disappointed when they found his partner was also a man, who was incidentally extremely effeminate and would strut about in the most astonishing way. His clothes were so tight they left nothing to the imagination whatsoever.

The flat Max eventually found had previously belonged to a rather talented interior designer and overlooked the Thames on the south side of the river. There were huge murals everywhere. The room I especially liked was the bathroom. There was a man, who rather reminded me of Charlie Chaplin, holding an umbrella standing underneath a rainbow which covered the whole wall under the shower and above the bath. It was a superior piece of artwork. Max had a passion for music. He enjoyed the more popular pieces of classical music and loved everything the Beatles had ever recorded as well as jazz and blues. The flat had huge hidden speakers everywhere. His favourite trick was to show unsuspecting guests to the toilet, wait until they were settled, and then play something – very loudly – through the speakers hidden there. It really used to startle people and amused him no end. The bedroom was enormous. It was beautifully decorated. The mural there covered the walls from floor to ceiling, comprising endless meadows carpeted with spring flowers of many colours. Along the skirting boards were blades of delicate green grass, no two alike. There were bees and butterflies, glittering jewels hovering around, and the artist had captured perfectly the morning dew suspended in silky webs from overnight spiders. I never tired of looking at it and each time would discover something new. The ceiling was, of course, a summer sky, palest blue with fluffy clouds and birds in flight swooping and soaring in the imaginary breeze. The carpet was white, soft and deep, delicious on bare feet. The furniture was also white, as were the curtains, billowing like sails. The room was dominated by a huge bed complete with white silk sheets and a silk-covered duvet. The kitchen was of a reasonable size, well equipped and always spotlessly clean, mostly pale wood with copper pans and utensils hanging from a rack suspended from the ceiling. Surprisingly, the lounge, compared to the bathroom and bedroom, was quite plain but comfortable. It was simply decorated in many shades of red, from the blood-red sofas, cerise cushions and burgundy carpet to the palest-pink walls. I spent many happy hours there listening to Max's vast music collection – mostly the Beatles and more especially 'Maybe I'm Amazed', which I absolutely loved and still do – drinking his wine and picking at the food he always prepared for me.

Alan came back from Lincolnshire and moved in with him, so I spent my time between two flats. It was during this time I discovered Max was actually bisexual. It hadn't occurred to me to wonder where Alan would sleep and was slightly shocked, but on reflection not surprised as he had always seemed slightly effeminate. We still saw each other, but it made a huge difference to how I felt about him. I didn't mind so much sharing him with other females, but this made me feel quite uncomfortable.

Whether it was as a result of the revelation of Max's sexual preferences or the general feel of the house, I was beginning to feel unsettled once again. Timothy and his boyfriend were still in residence and it was all becoming rather claustrophobic, although they were both very sweet and took great care of me.

Katy and I took off for a long weekend down on the Dorset coast as we both felt we needed a break. We were wandering along together when I saw a couple with a baby in a pushchair coming towards us. It was my sister! What a surprise! We could have picked anywhere, but chose that week and the very place where they were on their summer holiday!

Autumn had arrived. The days were dark, damp and depressing. Katy and Tony were fighting more and more, and eventually she decided to go back to her mother's for a while. She managed to get a transfer from her job and off she went. I missed her, but Tony was feeling absolutely bereft. After a long talk we decided to leave London together and move to a small town near Peterborough, where he had a flat. I rang the studio and explained I needed some time off, and they were very understanding and said they would keep my position open for a month or so before they advertised the vacancy. They had a collection for me – a very generous one – and bought me a rock of a ring from one of the upmarket jewellers close by. It resembled a screwed-up piece of kitchen foil with a small purple precious stone nestling in the folds, but was actually solid silver and extremely heavy to wear. It must have cost a small fortune!

We packed very little, as I presumed I would return shortly, but I hadn't given any thought to how long I would be away. I just felt relief to be escaping from the confines of the house and needed time to analyse my feelings for Max and to discover if my feelings for him outweighed his need for a boyfriend as well as me! I was also concerned for Tony as he was so obviously depressed, but realised he needed time away from Katy if their relationship was to be salvaged. I felt, not for the first time, there was no hope for their future together, but prayed I was wrong. So here we were, two lost souls together, both on an emotional rollercoaster. I was sure this time away together would benefit us both!

CHAPTER SIX

We left the following week and were soon rattling through the countryside. The buffet car was open, much to Tony's delight, and he soon found some travelling companions. They whiled away the journey playing cards and drinking while I watched the fields racing by. It took around an hour on the train, and with a short bus ride we were there. It was dark when we arrived, so I couldn't see much of the village. The flat was above a small grocery store. It was surprisingly spacious but sadly neglected. It comprised a lounge thickly carpeted, with two armchairs, a sideboard and an ancient coffee table which had definitely seen better days, an old-fashioned kitchen with dark oak cupboards and a very stained carpet, a reasonable-sized bathroom with a pink suite and two good bedrooms. I chose the smaller of the two. The ceiling had been painted in four huge triangles – two black and two bright pink, which Tony thought wouldn't make the room spin when one had had rather too much alcohol. The walls were painted in the same colours, but with bold stripes running horizontally around the room. His room was decorated in the same fashion, but in black and purple!

We had fortunately bought coffee, milk and sugar with us. Tony trotted off to the local chip shop and soon we were drinking hot coffee and eating our dinner wrapped in the previous week's news.

I found some rather grey-looking sheets and a blanket and crawled off to bed.

I slept really well and woke the next morning hearing voices beneath me, so I knew it was after nine o'clock and the shop was open. I slid out of bed and peered out of the window. I could see a narrow street with people chatting on doorsteps, very little traffic and, beyond, the countryside, stretching out as far as the eye could see. It was a beautiful day and the scene was bathed in sunshine.

I washed in cold water, dressed quickly, went to the kitchen and found two cleanish cups, made some coffee and went to find Tony. He was still asleep and it took much persuasion to rouse him.

We had to walk through the shop to reach the street. The lady behind the counter just nodded at Tony, glared at me and continued to pack groceries in a box for the customer who was standing there. I wanted to explore, but Tony was having none of it and we went straight to the pub.

It was very early, but he knocked smartly on the door and he was greeted with great enthusiasm and plied with his customary beverage. I drank quite a lot of wine and when we emerged I was somewhat wobbly.

More chips followed, which we ate sitting on an old stone bridge under a clear blue sky. The bridge was apparently extremely old, and it was quite famous. It looked out of place crouched there in the sunshine with no sign of water anywhere. If there once had been a river running beneath, it had dried up long ago. The village seemed mostly to be made up of four streets leading off from where we were, aptly named North Street, South Street, West Street and East Street.

We returned to the shop, to more frosty glances, bought more supplies (mostly cleaning materials) and returned to the flat. Tony stretched out to watch some television. He had lost the remote control some time ago and managed to change channels with a long section of bamboo. I tried to tidy up a little; the flat was in rather a sorry state and obviously hadn't been lived in for quite a long time. He had had someone to clean for him while he was there, but in his absence the flat had just been closed up and left. I still had some money from the studio, but if there was any work I decided I would take something temporary in case we stayed longer than planned.

We spent most of the following days in the local pub; it was the only one in the village and great fun. Most of the customers had a great time trying to decided what my relationship with Tony could be. The more they pried, the more evasive we became. In the end they gave up trying and I remained a mystery.

Most of the inhabitants knew him well and he had a constant stream of visitors. One afternoon a voice shouted up the stairs asking me if I was afraid of dogs. I wasn't. The man brought up two enormous wolfhounds; they were absolutely beautiful, but massive. He produced two washing-up bowls, two giant cans of food and a container of biscuits and began to shovel it all into the bowls; this is what they ate every day. They just opened their huge mouths and hoovered it up. They stayed for quite a while; but with the dogs asleep on the floor, and the three of us, it didn't leave a lot of space.

The local girls soon found Tony was back in residence. He was a good-looking and likeable chap and the girls couldn't resist him. His sadness began to lessen and he began to enjoy himself. He always referred to me as his housekeeper, and in fact this is how he started introducing me. It caused great hilarity between us. When one of his lady friends was in residence he would ring a little brass bell he kept on the coffee table. I would then duly appear dressed in black velvet hot pants (all the rage then), thigh-length leather lace-up boots, a very low-cut transparent lacy blouse, tiny frilly white pinny and a little lace cap. I carried a tray and, with a tea towel over my arm, I would give a little bob and ask what sir or madam required. This caused much merriment, and his visitors were never sure whether this was serious or we were just making fun of them. The expression on their faces was priceless.

I had a couple of casual boyfriends while I was there – nothing serious, just for company and somewhere else to go apart from the pub. One was the brother of Alan. He owned a powerful motorbike and he used to take me out perched on the back, excited but terrified, roaring through the countryside. One wet and windy night we were racing across the fens in excess of 100 miles an hour when a bridge loomed up ahead of us in the darkness. He slowed, but not enough. We hit a patch of ice. The bike went one way and we went another. Fortunately we landed in an extremely deep and muddy ditch. We escaped with cuts and bruises, but were very lucky. The bike was fine, so we climbed back on and drove slowly home. I didn't see him again after that. I realised what a lucky escape I'd had. Maybe the next time we wouldn't have been so fortunate, and I didn't want to chance it.

The next one I went out with was Trixie's brother. I had met him briefly when he came to visit her. He was very young and sweet and drove a dark-green sporty car which was easy to get into but awful to climb out of with any dignity. After Max's car it seemed small and slow, and he didn't understand why I wasn't impressed. He was good-humoured, generous and kindness itself, but I soon became bored with his company and saw him less and less until he stopped visiting altogether.

After a few weeks of lying around just eating chips and getting very drunk I was becoming bored and was running out of money, so I decided to get a job. There was a small employment agency in the village – just a front room of a house. If there was anyone there already, one had to wait in the street! Eventually I was seen and was offered a job packing vegetables in a factory about ten miles away. They were desperate for staff and the pay was reasonable, so I arranged to start the following morning. I had to get up at half past four to be ready in time to be picked up. We started at six o'clock, so I had to be ready to go at five.

It was dark and cold, but eventually a van came chugging along and stopped by the kerb beside me. The door creaked open and eager hands pulled me in. There was a cheery chorus of "Good morning" and we lurched off. They were a mixed bunch, but very jolly and friendly. It was hard to see where we were going as we trundled through the countryside, but we soon stopped and all scrambled out. I just followed everyone else and was left in a room to wait for the supervisor. She came bustling along and I was soon kitted out with a large overall, which was nearly down to the floor, an equally large apron, rubber gloves and wellington boots. I was also given a rather fetching hat, which was very similar to a shower cap. I was told to put all this on and she would return when I was ready. All the workers were supplied with a locker, so I undressed to my underwear and pulled on the clothes that had been provided for me. I must have looked quite a sight, but when she led me to the factory floor everyone was dressed in a similar fashion.

Soon I found myself standing by a huge conveyor belt, rolling along at an astonishing rate. The noise was amazing. Everyone seemed to be talking, or shouting, at once. I was on the cauliflower line that first day. The vegetables had come more or less straight from the fields, so had to be cleaned, trimmed, packed in Cellophane, boxed, labelled and sent to another section for distribution. I was very slow at first, but after a while could keep up with the others. The radio was on all the morning to add to the level of noise, but time passed quickly enough.

It was a huge factory and as the days passed I was moved around to different sections, wherever they were short-handed. During my time there I must have packed every vegetable imaginable. Bulbs were the worst of all. Apart from the fact they had to be counted, sometimes in quite large quantities, nobody liked working on that line. The dust from them made us itch horribly. Apparently if looked at under a microscope, the dust has tiny hooks, and these hooks dig into the skin and irritate it. I think it is called bulb rash. It was awful. The cold house was the next place that wouldn't win any prizes for popularity. It was very, very cold. Here was where all the frozen goods were fast-frozen and packed. Thankfully the shifts in there were deliberately shortened, so none of us had to remain in there for long periods of time.

Occasionally a shout would go up if one of the men from the banana sheds next door found an interesting insect (usually a spider or occasionally a brightly coloured beetle), unfortunately for the poor things quite dead. It would be brought into our area and the women who were scared of insects would be chased around, which really livened up the day. It's surprising how fast they ran in their rubber boots!

Tony would often disappear from time to time for a few days. He had a lot of shady deals going on – strange films, odd cigarettes, that kind of thing. I didn't know much about it really – not then, anyway. He did have a lot of friends; most of these were the local pillars of society. He regularly put on film shows (which I wasn't allowed to watch) and he liked me to be on the door in my housekeeping clothes to show his guests in. Sometimes there would be a change of plan and he would kit me out in winceyette pyjamas and fluffy slippers with curlers in my hair. I would be frantically knitting and had some very strange looks as his chosen audience sidled in avoiding my gaze and wandered up the stairs.

We spent that Christmas of 1970, just the two of us, in the flat. We exchanged gifts, then Tony kissed me for the first and only time. We used to fool around like a couple of kids.

I was quite happy with my little job and Tony had his little deals to keep him amused. As the weather turned even colder, and winter really began to bite, we piled all the bedding together on Tony's bed and cuddled up together beneath the blankets for warmth. As it turned colder still Tony covered me with his coat and tucked the blankets tightly around me. I felt safe and happy with him. It was a tranquil, peaceful time in my life.

But time marches on, and Tony at last felt he had had the break he needed and was missing the bright lights, parties, and more especially, Katy.

He mentioned returning to London: cautiously at first, but all in all things were pretty much against us. I now had my hours of work drastically reduced; in fact, my contract with the company had only weeks to run and I was afraid that soon I would have no hours at all. Tony's deals were by now very thin on the ground and, as he did not want to start digging into his investment interests, he suggested I stay until my work dried up altogether and he would go back to London and earn some quick cash. I could follow him when I was ready. Bills had by now started to arrive as it cost a fortune to keep the flat warm. I was very sad to see him wanting to return so desperately, but it was essential if we were to survive. We both felt very awkward with the situation, and he didn't want to leave me alone, but I woke one morning and found a short note saying he couldn't bear to say goodbye as he knew how distressed we would both be. He had gone!

I kept going for a few weeks, but the flat seemed so empty. After a fortnight the packing company laid us all off with the promise of work later in the spring. Two days after that the power was cut off. Tony obviously hadn't paid the bill! The flat was all electric, so it was difficult, to say the least. Apart from the occasional bag of chips, I lived on sandwiches and bowls of cereal. Washing in icy water wasn't my idea of fun, especially as the weather was so cold. I couldn't even boil a kettle. We had a lot of mice in the flat and they used to nibble their way into the cereal boxes and gnaw on the bread; it felt as if I had an army of lodgers and none of them contributed to the household budget! I couldn't even watch television or listen to any music – not that the stereo worked anyway! Tony had decided one evening in one of his drunken moments that the system wasn't getting into the spirit of things and tipped a pint of whisky and orange into its works. It was bitterly cold and I crawled into bed really early every night just to keep warm.

Life became very tedious, so one morning I decided to smarten myself up as best I could and walk into Peterborough. It was a total of eighteen miles there and back, but it kept me warm. I was wandering around when I saw a job advertised in an optician's window for a receptionist. I had done a huge amount of this kind of work, so in I went. After a short interview they took me on being very impressed with my experience in London. The salary was quite a bit more than I was earning in the factory, so I was able to eat and pay off the electricity bill. The phone was still off, but I thought I could do without that for the time being.

It was good to be working again. The job was rather boring and the other girls there weren't friendly at all, but it didn't bother me. While I was working there decimal currency came in, so I know it was February 1971. It caused a lot of confusion, especially among the elderly, but we all soon became familiar with it. Time drifted along. It was good sitting in a café I had found close to my work at lunchtime with a plate of hot food in front of me, watching the world go by. I joined the local library as well, so had lots of books to read, which was rather a struggle at first by candlelight, but I managed quite well. I suppose I must have been quite lonely, but was reasonably content. With my first week's salary I managed to pay the outstanding bill, so once again had light and hot water. The first thing I did was run a bath – absolute bliss! Sitting propped up in bed with light and a book, after managing with the meagre glow from spluttering candles, was a joy. I didn't have a lot of food in the flat, but was eating a hot meal every day in the café in Peterborough.

I still missed Tony, but continued to go to the pub when the appeal of some human company drove me out of the flat. There was a boy there, Paul, who had paid me a lot of attention in the past and once he knew Tony had left he paid me more attention still. He started to call round, and it wasn't long before he was there all the time. He didn't like me to see anyone else, to go to work (but of course it was essential), to read or to watch television (unless it was a programme he decided was suitable), and he started to become very aggressive. The aggression soon turned to violence and he started to hit me. It just became a living nightmare. He used to pin me against the wall by my throat and slap me repeatedly if he thought I had been talking to someone in the pub for too long. He then began to beat me with his fists, but was very careful to aim his blows where the marks wouldn't show.

This went on for some time until one night he went off to the pub alone in a temper and left me in peace. Some hours later I heard footsteps on the stairs and tensed, waiting for the next beating I knew would come as by now Paul would have been drinking steadily for quite a while. I shrank back, shaking with fear, and Tony's head appeared. He knew something was wrong as soon as he saw me. He was so angry. He stood in the middle of the lounge yelling at me at the top of his voice. I think it was partly guilt at leaving, and he had been frantic with worry because he hadn't heard from me. He stripped me off, gasping at the damage Paul had inflicted on my battered body, laid me in a warm bath, washed me gently like a baby, dried me and put me to bed. Then he went off to the pub to find Paul. I don't know what happened and was never told, but I think Paul must have left the area in a great hurry because to my knowledge he wasn't seen again. Tony returned within fifteen minutes, still shaken with shock and horror at what had happened to me in his absence. He was upset because I hadn't rung and told him what was going on. I explained that I had been too afraid because Paul had threatened to kill me if I told anyone what was happening; besides, the phone was off and the one in the village hadn't worked for some time.

Tony stayed with me then until my bruises faded and I felt less nervous and jumpy. When he felt I had recovered somewhat he came on the bus with me to work to hand in my notice, swearing he would never leave me alone up there again. I protested, but once Tony had made up his mind about something nothing would shift him. We went back to the flat and he packed for me.

By the time we had finished shouting at each other it was rather late. We had missed the last bus, and the last train as well, so walked the nine miles and waited in the station until the early morning train pulled in.

CHAPTER SEVEN

On the train Tony thought of a brilliant idea. When we arrived in London he hailed a cab and we climbed into the back, where we proceeded to get undressed, which proved quite difficult in such a confined space. How the driver managed to stay on the road I don't know, he was laughing so much. At the next set of traffic lights he turned around to have a good look at what he thought would be two people in a passionate clinch, only to find us sitting primly dressed in pyjamas. It took him a long time to recover his composure and pull away from the lights when they turned green. When we arrived at the house he refused to take any money for our fare, saying we had given him one of the best laughs he had had for ages.

Tony rang all the bells and we sat on the doorstep to wait. Eventually we heard footsteps and a sleepy figure peered round the door at us. Tony had saved a small plastic cup from the train journey and he solemnly held it out and asked if we could possibly borrow a cup of sugar as the shop under the flat was closed. What an uproar we caused. Soon everyone in the house was up and crowding around the door to see what all the fuss was about. We were carried shoulder-high through the hallway and up the stairs. Everyone had, of course, thought we were miles away tucked up in our beds, not zooming around London in the early hours dressed in pyjamas looking for sugar!

Amazingly Katy was there, having come for a visit to see everyone, and she was dumbstruck. I looked at them gazing at each other and thought they were two of the people I loved most in the world. I hoped desperately that the time apart had healed the rift and they would be together again once more.

We moved in with Trixie on the second floor. The sofa bed had mysteriously vanished and nobody in the house had any idea what had happened to it. We slept in sleeping bags, which wasn't very comfortable, but were so delighted to be together again it didn't bother us one bit. Timothy and his boyfriend had moved on by now and had found themselves another apartment a few blocks down from the one they had recently sold. The recent events still had me feeling nervous and somewhat fragile, so it was decided I should just stay in the flat, sleep and try to put the whole business behind me. Katy meanwhile had found a job in one of the up-and-coming boutiques that were springing up all over London. Life settled down again. We didn't socialise much. We were quite happy with one another's company and would spend the evenings sitting in our private green oasis under the trees. It was spring again, days were lengthening and the weather was becoming warmer once more. The gardens were a much needed private space, and always peaceful. We would sit on the bench listening to the sighing of leaves and the rustling of creatures in the undergrowth, speaking of our hopes and dreams. Late in the evening the owls would call. My experience with Paul had left me shaken and I wondered if I would ever trust again. I knew Max was not going to be the one – the love of my life – but I still missed him, and because I knew him well I felt safe and secure with him. Katy felt the same about Tony, although she felt her time with him was coming to an end. She didn't know if she wanted to get off the roundabout that had become her relationship with him or 'buy another ticket' and go round again!

Summer arrived and we decided to visit a new wine bar that had opened up around the corner from us. We tidied ourselves up, which involved simply pulling on clean jeans, and trotted off arm in arm down the street. The bar had previously been a rather run-down pub, but it had been spruced up and looked very attractive from the outside so in we went. To our amazement

Tony was there with two of the hairiest men I had ever seen. Introductions were made. Apparently they were a couple of Irish lads who had just become homeless and Tony thought he might be able somehow to squeeze them into the house with us. They were gorgeous! Joseph was tall, dark and very funny. But Peter! He had blonde hair, and the lights from the bar behind him turned it into a golden halo. He had the bluest, gentlest eyes and such a kind face. There was an instant rapport between us. We agreed that they could come back to the flat and we would find a place for them there. Tony told Katy one of his tenants had moved on and left empty property and he wanted to have one last chance, which she hastily agreed to, not able to resist another opportunity to be with him. We took the boys home and Katy left with Tony to see the place he had found.

Space was now rather cramped again, but I knew Katy would be leaving. Robyn had by now found two girls, who were both Londoners, to share the top floor with her. The bedsits were small, but Arthur took a liking to Joseph and he moved in with him, which left Peter. It didn't take me long to decide, rather foolishly as it turned out, to invite him to share the flat with Trixie and me, the sleeping arrangements being Trixie in her own room and Peter and me sharing the front room. We acquired a double mattress from somewhere and he soon settled in. I thought I had at last found the man I had been looking for. Within weeks he had asked me for my hand in marriage and we started to make arrangements. The church where I had been christened was chosen as the venue and a date was fixed for the following spring, 1972. I chose a dress, told both sets of parents and settled down to wait for the big day. Why did I do it? I can only think it was some kind of madness – a safe haven away from Paul or some sort of rebound after all the highs and lows of the wonderful Max.

Trixie could see what was going on and persuaded me to go home with her one weekend to see her family. She hoped to talk some sense into me. I didn't want to leave him, but she was most insistent, so off we went. We attracted a lot of attention, bouncing along northwards towards her home. Her little car was certainly bright and very noticeable. It reminded me of Noddy's car (bright yellow with red wheels). The car was quite elderly and not familiar with long journeys. It grew very hot and bothered, and after numerous stops, where she would cough and wheeze until she cooled down sufficiently for us continue, we pulled up outside Trixie's family home – or, rather, family seat!

I was amazed at the size of the place. It was huge. Originally a substantial old farmhouse, it had been converted to an extremely comfortable family home which still retained the charm of the original building. Downstairs there was a huge family kitchen with scrubbed pine table and an Aga, three living rooms, a formal dining room and a cloakroom; upstairs there were eight bedrooms and two bathrooms. Her parents were very welcoming and after showing me to my room announced they were having a party that evening, in the attic! I imagined an attic similar to the one we had in London, but it actually ran the whole length of the house and was furnished with rugs on polished floorboards and shabby squashy sofas.

After a welcome cup of coffee and some delicious homemade biscuits, Trixie and I were sent off to the woods, which were part of their land, to gather firewood. We had to cross several fields to reach them and in one was a herd of cows. Now, I'm a town girl through and through, and of course cows are nosy and very large. They began to walk towards us and I just ran, back to and over the gate in true Olympic style. Trixie laughed so hard that she sat on the ground with a thump, tears rolling down her face. But I had been genuinely afraid and she had to collect the logs on her own as I refused to cross the field again.

Lunch was served quite informally in the kitchen: a full roast dinner, with apple pie and custard to follow. There was much talk and laughter.

A relaxing afternoon was spent, playing cards with Trixie's father, who cheated shamelessly but was instantly forgiven; he was obviously so close to his daughter and thrilled to see her so unexpectedly.

The party was a huge success. A buffet had been laid on,

which we all had a hand in, and there were barrels of beer and crates of wine. The boys that had shared the house with Tony and Max were there as well as Trixie's brother, who understandably was polite but distant. It carried on until the early hours.

When I finally reached my bed I was exhausted, but I didn't sleep at all, I was so cold. Although it was only late summer there was a definite chill in the air and I couldn't get warm at all.

After a rather large breakfast we were soon bouncing back to London. Trixie tried so hard over that weekend to persuade me to rethink my plans, but I was adamant that I knew what I was doing. We chatted about other things then, as we chugged along again with the frequent stops for the car to recover. We decided during the journey that, as some of the tenants of that wonderful house were working and others not, it would be a great idea to pool resources! Those that worked brought home the bacon, as it were, and the rest cooked, cleaned, did the laundry and generally made life easier.

Eventually, after what seemed a very long time, we ground to a halt outside the house and I'm sure I heard the car give a sigh of relief. I rushed in to see Peter, so pleased we were reunited and swearing we would never be apart again.

We implemented our grand plan the following week and it worked like a charm. It was great to return from work to a hot meal, a clean house and clothes washed and pressed. I visited the art studio to see if my position was still open, but they had unfortunately found someone else so I decided to return to temping for a while.

Trixie and Katy had decided between them that time apart from Peter yet again was a good plan, and a holiday was secretly and swiftly arranged without my knowledge. A friend of Trixie's mother had a small caravan in the heart of Somerset, and it was duly borrowed for the following week. When the day came I was dragged out of bed and carried protesting to Trixie's little car and we chugged off. I presume a note was left for Peter, but it wasn't discussed.

When we arrived we found a very dilapidated caravan, which had been hand-painted (not very well, I might add!) in a muddy cream and dark-green gloss paint, sitting forlornly under a hedge on the edge of a rather muddy field. The interior wasn't much better, but it was dry and clean. By then I had cheered up immensely and didn't mind one bit! There was nobody around to bother us and we spent a glorious week high on alcohol and drugs. I was still adamant I was going to marry Peter, and in the end they gave up trying to change my mind. Soon we were on our way back to London, all very tired and grubby but happy to be going home.

After a couple of days catching up on sleep and spending time with Peter, I knew I had to look for work again. One of the jobs on offer was as a tea lady in the famous store where Tony's friend worked. We had rather a grand uniform: navy dress with the company logo picked out in fancy gold lettering, navy shoes and a very strange hat which appeared to be made of stiff paper. I had to pin it to my hair to ensure it stayed on. There wasn't room in the lift for me and the tea trolley, so I would push it in laden with tea urn, cups and saucers and an assortment of biscuits, press the button for the appropriate floor then rush either up or down the stairs to meet the trolley as the doors opened. This only lasted about a month; rushing up and down stairs became very tiring, so I looked for something else.

It was by now nearly Christmas once more and there was seasonal work to be had in most of the large stores around London. There was also office work to be found, but I discovered there was a vacancy back in the chemist; so back I went, serving this time on the maternity counter. The uniformed nannies would come in with their precious charges in high prams. We sold everything a baby could possibly need, including some very expensive designer clothing.

The wedding arrangements were still going well, but Peter didn't seem to be spending much time in the flat with me. He seemed very preoccupied. By now he had started to become heavily into the drug scene along with Dave. Sandra wasn't very happy about it, but in her quiet way tolerated the situation and hoped it would pass.

Christmas came and went and suddenly it was New Year's Eve. Dave unfortunately took what we presumed was a hallucinogenic drug (so freely available at the time) and jumped out of the bathroom window, believing he could fly. We all rushed outside, fearing the worst, but although he was bleeding badly he didn't appear to be seriously injured. We summoned an ambulance, which quickly arrived. They were marvellous, checked him over, decided he needed stitches to a deep cut on his forearm and took him away. He was also very badly bruised and the hospital decided to keep him overnight for observation. He must have been so relaxed when he fell that he didn't hurt himself badly. We were all obviously extremely upset and talked long into the night.

Suddenly we realised Peter was not to be found. Trixie went to search for him and found him in Sandra's bed! In his charming Irish way he had persuaded her he could help her pass the time until Dave's return. Trixie was so angry with them both. She asked Peter to leave immediately, slapped Sandra hard and stormed back to me. When she told me what she had found I was horrified. I just wanted to run away from the house and the people. She packed what belongings she could squeeze into her car. Then she sat me in the passenger seat and once again I was on the way back to my parents.

CHAPTER EIGHT

They were extremely sympathetic, but I think rather pleased that it had made me come to my senses. Whatever possessed me to agree to that marriage I will never know. I knew absolutely nothing about him, and had never met his family or friends. Madness! I was, of course, extremely upset for a long time, but eventually began to put the pieces back together and tried to decide what to do next. I was sad to leave our lovely house, but knew I could never return. It just wouldn't feel the same any more.

I did go and visit Tony and Katy in their new home, however. It was in a very exclusive block further west than we had been living and very quiet. The rooms were large with high ceilings; the windows were tall panes of glass, flooding the flat with light. The kitchen was very modern, all chrome and black, and the bathroom and bedrooms were equally impressive. I sensed, however, a tension between Tony and Katy – nothing definite, just a strange atmosphere as if they were somehow acting the part. I hoped desperately they would stay together, but I felt that it really was the beginning of the end for them this time. I prayed I was wrong.

Back at my parents' house the days drifted by. The days turned to weeks, and then it was spring again. The date we had set for the wedding arrived. I wanted to talk to Peter, but had no idea where he was. I still wasn't working – I couldn't face getting up in the mornings and fighting to get on the Underground and off it again, so mostly stayed in bed reading or sleeping. Time passed by and the approaching summer seemed to give me hope and energy once more. I spent my days not hiding away, but striding through the local park or gardening enthusiastically. I felt revived and my old energy was returning.

Once again early one morning the shrill of the doorbell woke me and I stumbled downstairs to be greeted by the sight of a very dishevelled Katy in tears standing on the doorstep. It seemed she and Tony had finally come to the end of the road. She was distraught. I tucked her into my bed and she finally cried herself to sleep. My parents were, by now, completely bewildered and probably wondering why we couldn't just find some 'nice' boys and settle down.

After Katy had slept and recovered slightly she begged me to go away with her – far, far away. She just wanted a fresh start. The idea appealed to me very much, and once again we went out and bought the newspapers. Of course all the flats and jobs were in London or the local area and we didn't want that, so we found a map. Katy shut her eyes and stabbed at it with a pin, opened them again and we were staring at Devon. Well, why not! My poor parents would have suggested the moon by this stage, so we were once again launching ourselves into the future, hoping that this time we could leave all the heartache we had both experienced behind us and start afresh. A map of Devon was obtained from the local library and a town by the sea was decided upon.

We decide to travel by coach as it was the cheapest option. Katy gave in her notice at the boutique and I rang the chemist and told them I wouldn't be back. We packed what we thought were the basics. We had a small bag each and a rucksack, sleeping bags and the clothes on our backs, and that was it. It was an uneventful journey and we didn't speak much, both lost in our thoughts of what might have been. I think we changed buses at some point on our journey, but I can't be sure. It was hours later when we found ourselves on the local bus weaving through country lanes while we peered over the hedges at the scenery as it flashed by. The bus chugged into what was laughingly called a coach station (three bus stops and two seats) and ground to a halt, and we tumbled out, stretching our aching limbs.

The first step, we decided, was to find somewhere to live, so while I sat on one of the seats there, with our belongings scattered around me, Katy went off to buy a local newspaper. When she returned we went to a nearby café and sat down to look for accommodation. It was early evening by this time, so we knew we would have to hurry or sleep on the beach for the night! There were a few likely ones, but it was by now early summer and most of the rental property had been snapped up by tourists wanting their week or so in the sun. The one we liked the sound of was 'Beach Villa' (it seemed to have a continental ring to it), and after asking a passer-by for directions we found it easily enough. Standing outside the property we stared in disbelief. It was a two-storey building with an overgrown garden circling it. The walls, which had originally been painted white, were now grey and crumbling. The paint around the door and windows was black – or, indeed, what was left of the paintwork as that too was faded in places and flaking badly. It hardly looked continental; it was rather sad and neglected. We hammered on the door carefully – there was no bell and we didn't want to take the door off its rusty hinges. Eventually a small wizened old man shuffled into view. He looked very cross at being disturbed and it took a lot of shouting and pointing to the advertisement in the paper before he realised what we had come for. He was very deaf, which in the following months would indeed be a blessing.

Katy with that way of hers soon took over and when she waved money at him we found ourselves inside the house. He explained – rather loudly – that he lived on the ground floor and let the upstairs. He led us into his apartment, as he called it, and it was incredible. He said he had been an antique dealer before he retired some years previously. What chaos it was! He had a camp bed and there was a small cooker in the corner of the room, but the rest of the space was piled high with everything imaginable – lots of rolled rugs, old chairs, paintings, crockery, lamps, boxes overflowing with tarnished jewellery, and old newspapers everywhere.

Katy soon had the key and we rushed off to see the flat. The wallpaper on the stairs was peeling and the carpet was threadbare, but we were so excited. We opened the flat door and stood there open-mouthed. The door led straight into a small kitchen which was filthy, with cracked linoleum covering the floor. A greasy cooker stood in one corner and a beautiful old-fashioned and scratched dresser stood along the wall. On the other side of the room was a small glass-fronted cupboard with oddments of chipped crockery, a few pots and pans and some stained cutlery. There was also a small fridge. An archway from the kitchen led into the main room, which held two single beds, an armchair and a small built-in wardrobe. There were French doors leading to a balcony, and through these we could see the blue sea sparkling in the sunset. Tugging them, we stepped outside and could hear the sea crashing on the rocks far below us. The view was breathtaking. Countryside on either side of us as far as the eye could see was punctuated by tiny houses and animals in fields. We were delighted with it all. What we needed now was a job – or, in fact, two jobs – then life would once again have some meaning and structure to it.

We didn't take long to unpack. The old gent had given us some sheets and blankets which looked clean enough, so we made up the beds. We boiled some water and found some scraps of soap in the bathroom down the hall, and, with a scrubbing brush Katy had found, we smartened the place up as best we could, then sat up in bed making a list of things we would have to buy the following day to make our little flat into something resembling a home. We fell asleep quickly. It must have been all that fresh country air in our lungs, those sea breezes blowing through the French windows we couldn't bear to close and the sound and rhythm of the sea.

The next morning we dragged the chair out on to the balcony and I sat at Katy's feet while we had our breakfast. She had her usual Liquorice Allsorts and I had some biscuits and an apple left from our journey the day before.

We then dressed and set off to explore, to see if we could find some sort of employment to keep a roof over our heads and food in our stomachs. We decided it was probably better to separate. Katy headed off up the High Street and I wandered in the direction of the harbour, where I stopped for a while and watched the boats bobbing in the sunshine and listened to the gulls crying overhead. I soon came across a large hotel with a card in the window asking for staff, so in I went. After a few questions the job of a waitress was mine, and after promising to buy something suitable to wear and agreeing to be there at seven o'clock the next morning I was back out in the sun again. Not far from the hotel was a department store, and I soon emerged with some black shoes, a short black dress and a white apron. Feeling extremely pleased with myself, I made my way to the café we had visited the day before and sat down to wait for Katy. I didn't have a long wait before I saw her running down the road towards me. She had also found a job (at a bookmaker's she had seen from the bus on our way into the town). As she had previous experience they welcomed her with open arms. She didn't have to start until the following week, so it was decided that she would do any necessary decorating while I made some money. The rest of that day we explored and generally lazed in the sun. We were both rather stunned that it had all happened so quickly. A new town, new home and a new job in a matter of hours! We were determined to succeed and congratulated each other on our good fortune.

The next morning I presented myself at the hotel suitably attired to start my new job. It was a fairly large establishment and the dining room was enormous. There were only three of us waiting on: me, the boss's daughter and her best friend. We each had our own workstations, so really all I had to do was learn to carry armfuls of hot plates and remember what each guest had ordered. Speed was of the essence. Fortunately there was one door out of the kitchen and a different one back in, so there was no danger of falling over one another. It was extremely hot and it took me quite a few weeks to get used to it.

Most of the guests were fine (they were on holiday, relaxed and friendly), but there's always one, as they say; and one in particular has stuck in my mind. It was the beginning of her holiday – I think the first or second day. She whined and complained about everything. On that particular morning I asked what she would like to order for breakfast, and she decided kippers and custard would be rather good. Of course the customer is always right! All the other guests, both at her table and at the surrounding ones, thought this was highly amusing. I trotted off to the kitchen and asked the chef if we had any instant custard. Into the store cupboard we went – and yes, we did. I grabbed a kipper, popped it in a dish and poured hot water on the custard powder, which was added and returned to her table. She was speechless! The whole dining room erupted in applause as they could see how difficult she had been.

She was to stay for two weeks, and as the days passed I got to know her. She was in fact psychic – a medium! One day she offered me a reading after my shift. I met her in a quiet corner after work and she told me, amongst other things, that I would marry twice! Considering I didn't intend to marry at all, I was somewhat taken aback. After that she was very sweet to me and at the end of her stay left me a very large tip.

Katy was busy in the flat, wallpapering and painting. It was beginning to look very homely and welcoming. I now had some cash, so we decided to treat ourselves to an evening out. On our explorations round the town we had seen some handwritten posters advertising a folk club, so we thought we would go along and see what it was like.

We didn't know what to expect at all. It was being held in a large building, not unlike a corrugated shed, and it was packed to the rafters. Rows and rows of people were sitting in circles on old, rickety chairs. We managed to find two spare seats and sat down. A very tall man with shoulder-length greasy hair and dark glasses, carrying a guitar, ambled in followed by a tiny dark girl in what I can only describe as a long flannelette nightie. The room fell silent and he began to play. What followed was haunting. Those two insignificant people seemed to grow before our eyes. She had one of the purest, sweetest voices I have ever heard and his playing accompanying her was so intimate it was like an intrusion. When they had finished their set – to thunderous applause, I may add – another insignificant man came shuffling on and broke the spell the audience were under only to cast another. His songs weren't haunting, but unaccompanied and melodious. After a while he too finished and we were surrounded by many bearded and sandalled men, so we made our escape. We felt quite euphoric and decided this was well worth another visit.

We went there about six times in all. On what was to become our final visit, the greasy, long-haired man and one of his friends decided to come home with us, and after consuming rather a lot of wine they decided they might stay the night! The friend took off his shirt, and where his unwashed body had perspired rather freely the dye from the blue shirt had run into his skin. The greasy, long-haired chap was equally – shall we say? – unsavoury, in the same way, and they were soon shown the door. We stopped going there after that. Dirty unwashed bodies are definitely not on the list of the requirements that make a man attractive.

We then found a lively pub we preferred, a short stroll through a tiny shopping arcade next to our new home, and spent most of our evenings there when we weren't working. It was a wild place, busy every night. All the locals sat at one end – fishermen, labourers and suchlike, big, tough, beefy men. All the seasonal workers and holidaymakers congregated at the other end and there was a sort of no-man's-land in between. If there was any trouble, the locals used to move as one body and throw the offender out – usually through the door, but occasionally straight through the window. It must have cost a fortune to replace the glass time and time again. We loved it – the noise, the atmosphere of the place and especially the landlord! He was extremely handsome (and knew it) – smouldering brown eyes, dark and very tall. His wife was very quiet and nervous. Eventually as the summer season progressed the strain began to tell and they parted. He bought her a house at the other end of town, but after a brief stay there and an attempt at reconciliation she took the children and returned to her parents, who, I think, lived in Mid Devon.

Time passed swiftly and suddenly it was October 1972, the end of the season, and I was out of a job. There was fortunately an employment centre in the town; it was packed with seasonal workers hoping to find employment so they could stay for the winter. The only work available was a receptionist in a solicitor's office, so I was forced to accept it if we were to stay in the flat and eat. I started the following week, but was not happy there at all. They were all very prim and proper, but I had a job.

Katy was still pining for Tony, so was overjoyed to receive a letter from him asking if he could come and stay with us for a weekend. We were waiting for them to arrive when we heard the sound of a car and peered out of the window. It was a blue Morgan and out climbed Tony and Max. I was delighted to see them both again. They were both very impressed with our flat, jobs and lifestyle; and I think they were a little jealous of this apparently peaceful life we had found. Although it was so good to see them, Katy and I felt we had to move on at last and could now look on them as dear friends.

I had a boyfriend by then, George, but like Max in the past he used to give me the runaround. He drove a black Jaguar and had an adorable boxer dog called Cassius. He loved that dog more than anything else, but he took him up on the cliffs one day for a run and Cassius simply vanished. Whether someone took him or he fell over the edge nobody ever knew.

Max was keen to renew our earlier passion, but with George sitting in the corner glowering at us both I decided it wasn't a good idea and Max accepted the situation with good grace.

We decided that weekend to hold a party for our guests to meet the new friends we had made. We asked the landlord's permission and the answer was a firm no, but we weren't going to be put off that easily. We had previously spotted a ladder lying amongst the weeds in the garden, and now we crept out and borrowed it. We propped it against the balcony and our friends started to climb up. The landlord was so deaf that he didn't hear a thing, and after much shuffling and whispering we managed to get them all in. I don't know how many people we had there, but it was quite a squeeze. Everyone drank so much they were quite unable to return the way they had come, so they all stayed and we partied on through the night and most of the following day.

Max and Tony returned to London early the following week and life went on.

Katy had started to visit her mother once again, at first occasionally then every weekend she could. At the time I didn't think anything untoward was happening, but after one visit she sat me down and announced she was pregnant! She had apparently been seeing someone casually on her visits home and, although the pregnancy wasn't planned, she was delighted and the father of the child wanted to be with her. She intended to leave the very next day. Her news was a complete bombshell – a huge shock. I had no idea she was seeing anybody! I was so worried about her, about whether the boy would stay with her and about how she was going to bring up a child alone if he left. We talked long into the night. I planned to see the landlord the next day to explain my predicament and see if I could cook or clean for him in return for a reduction in the rent.

We both slept badly and the morning came all too soon. I waved her off from that same coach station where we had arrived full of hopes and dreams, then I returned to the flat, threw myself on the bed and howled. I knew how much I would miss her, but she now had a whole new future before her and I had to pick up the pieces and carry on.

The next few days passed in a fog. The landlord was fortunately very understanding and just asked for the occasional meal and halved the rent! I was so relieved. The next few days were spent in a kind of limbo. I was very lonely without her and I prayed she would be happy. I knew how she really felt about Tony, but it obviously wasn't meant to be. I still hated my job, but it paid well, I had made some good friends and life carried on.

A week before Christmas I had a decision to make, whether to go and visit my parents or go and see Katy. From her letter she sounded as lonely as I was, so a bag was packed and off to the bus station I went. She had found herself a flat, but at that time was living alone. It was more of a bedsit than a flat – a large room with a bed and a sofa at one end and a small kitchenette at the other, with a bathroom on the floor below. It suited Katy for the present, however, as she hadn't decided whether to move to Bristol, where the father of the child she was carrying originated from, or to stay close to her mother.

The flat was on the top floor (where else!) of a crumbling building opposite a nightclub. The noise after dark was incredible. On the wall hung a neon sign, which flashed on and off continuously. It was very strange trying to sleep with the room illuminated first in yellow, then red and back again.

We had a picnic on a blanket for our Christmas lunch – cold turkey and salad, cheese and fruit all washed down with wine, which I admit I drank most of because Katy was concerned for the health of the child growing inside her. I did toy with the idea of moving to be near her, but Bristol wasn't where I wanted to live, and although the Sussex coast was attractive in its own way it seemed to be always noisy and busy. I was beginning to become homesick for Devon. I realised how much I disliked my job, however, and because I couldn't bear to leave Katy I stayed well into the New Year so I knew that when I returned the job wouldn't be there any more anyway. We parted with the promise of meeting up again in the not too distant future, and it was with a heavy heart that I returned home.

The flat seemed so cold and empty. I threw my bag down and slumped on the bed with a huge sigh. Where from here? Fortunately I had some remarkable friends and a small amount of money, so for a few weeks, at least until I had to think about working again, I could relax.

The couple I started to spend a lot of time with were living just across the hallway. They reminded me very much of Dave and Sandra from the house in London. They lived quietly, were also vegetarians and he was very blonde, she very dark. They were extremely comforting to be with, hadn't the need to fill silent spaces with endless pointless chatter and watched over me as I came to terms with Katy's departure. They fed me fruit, brown rice and vegetables most days, played my favourite songs and laughed and cried with me until the misery eased. They also had a wide circle of friends and through them I met a different crowd of people. They all smoked a lot of cannabis resin and after a while I fell into their habits. It eased the pain and loneliness I felt, and after some time I began to dress in the same manner too. We all wore long caftans. I remember two of them: one was black one side with a white sleeve and the opposite on the other side; the other was green velvet covered in small mirrors. We all had very long hair (even the boys), rarely wore shoes and when not in either their flat or mine we would go for long walks together over the cliffs to buy more supplies from their dealer friends, who lived in splendid isolation in a fisherman's cottage high above the town; then there would be the long walk home again. It was a strange period in my life. I was one person by day and then completely different when evening came. We were frequently stopped by the local constabulary, when we would discreetly hurl small packages into the undergrowth, but they were very friendly and knew us all well.

It was now early June and my birthday arrived. I wanted to spend it quietly and alone, so I rose early, crept out of the flat and wandered down to the harbour, where I caught the steamer to an island just off the coast, I had a perfect day wandering around with soft grass underfoot, the wide sky above me and the sound of the sea and the gulls. There was wildlife to find, and I spent hours just sitting and watching quietly. I had packed a picnic for myself – mostly small boxes of salad and fruit and small bottles of juice, cool and refreshing in the summer sun. Regretfully it was soon time to leave and I stood on the deck of the steamer watching the island become smaller and smaller behind me.

My friends and neighbours had realised it was my birthday because of the amount of cards the postman had brought that morning, and they decided to have a party in my honour. It was this I returned to. Half of the town must have been there, but I'd had no inkling at all, although somebody must have been very busy rushing around rounding everybody up! What an event! It lasted three days, and at one point I was apparently (although I do not remember it!) sitting under a coffee table playing a particular card game and winning. I have not played that game either before or since and do not know how I managed it at all.

Eventually the flat was empty again, and although Katy was very much on my mind I felt comforted by the number of good friends I had made since living there.

The nights had turned milder now and I sometimes dragged my mattress on to the balcony and slept under the stars, drifting off to the sound of the sea, or I would stroll down the hill to a small cove I had discovered and sleep on the sand, taking a rod with me to catch fish as the dawn came up.

CHAPTER NINE

Although I couldn't afford to go out much I decided the following week to have a night out in the pub. I was still really miserable without Katy and thought it would cheer me up. I dressed in jeans and T-shirt and wore sandals. I didn't think the clientele in the pub would appreciate a caftan and dirty feet! The pub was packed as usual, but I squeezed in at the locals' end (which I considered myself now to be) and found a stool at the corner of the bar. Poor Nick (that gorgeous landlord) was rushing around in a state of near panic. One of his female staff had walked out because she couldn't take the aggravation any more and the girl working that night was fairly new and very flustered. Nick saw me sitting there and something must have clicked in his fuddled brain! He galloped round to my side of the bar, picked me up to a huge cheer and ran round behind the bar again with me still in his arms. Then he put me gently on my feet, took my bag from me and stowed it in a corner and informed me I was now a barmaid. I was a regular customer and he knew me well enough to know I was honest, wouldn't pocket the takings and certainly wouldn't take any nonsense from anyone.

I ran up and down behind that bar for what seemed like hours until the bell for last orders was rung, then I was given the honour of emptying the pub, the theory being that customers are less likely to cause trouble if they are asked to leave by a woman. That night it worked like a dream. Of course there were other duties as well. I objected to going downstairs to the gents' toilets to see how many bodies were to be found. It was revolting down there.

After everyone had left and we had washed all the glasses and tidied up (the cleaners would finish it in the morning), and the other barmaid had gone home, Nick sat me down with a glass of chilled wine and asked me what I thought. I realised I hadn't enjoyed myself so much for a long time, and he offered me a full-time job there and then. The money wasn't much, but it was like being paid for a night out with more room! We talked for a long time. Underneath that brash 'mine host' exterior he was just like a lost little boy. He missed his wife; and although they had come to an arrangement where he would see the children, he felt their loss greatly.

I felt a lot happier as I quietly let myself into the flat that night, and I slept well.

The weeks that followed were a joy. It was such fun working in the pub. The time passed quickly as it was so very busy. There was always someone wanting to start a fight, and I was usually despatched to sort it out, the theory being that if a woman gets in between quarrellers, they won't hit her. In all the time I was there I didn't get even a scratch, and the locals were very protective towards me and alert for any disturbance that might occur.

Only one night did I make a small misjudgement and asked someone to leave who had been drinking heavily. He picked up a bar stool and threw it at me. I ducked and it missed me by inches. He left the bar rather more swiftly than he had entered, through the window! I was rather pleased because I had never liked him very much anyway, and he was banned for life. The locals were horrified and crowded round me to make sure I wasn't hurt. Wendy, his girlfriend, who had been with him, kept apologising on his behalf, although it wasn't her fault at all. She was Welsh, small and blonde with a daft dog of doubtful breeding called Charley. She came into the pub alone after that, and we developed quite a close friendship.

I was still spending much of my spare time with my neighbours and new-found friends. We had some amazing nights out together. On one occasion we all decided to take a popular little tablet (the one which had encouraged Dave in London to try flight!) and went off to a party being held in a large room above one of the other pubs in the town. The ceiling above our heads had been decorated with luminous stars, and the walls were draped in dark-blue material, dotted with small green men. None of us knew it was fancy dress and that the waiters would be dressed as spacemen and the guests as assorted Martians and monsters! I walked in first and when I turned to see what their reaction was they all thought they were hallucinating and took flight. I was left alone. It was a strange experience and one I will never forget.

Another couple who became close friends lived in an upstairs flat just around the corner from me. I remember visiting them and *The Old Grey Whistle Test* always seemed to be on the television. We loved it. They had no furniture in their living room, just cushions and a fibre-optic lamp in the centre of the room. We would all sit around the lamp, glazed and silent, watching the colours change and change back again.

Other friends, also close by, had a flat with a long balcony overlooking the sea, with room enough for several armchairs, and many a night I would be there nursing a glass of wine watching the sun come up.

Yet more friends lived in a converted church. The front door led into a very large square room – again not much furniture, but large cushions, which we all favoured. There were wooden stairs on either side of the room, leading to a balcony which circled the room below completely. Off this were the bedrooms (six in all) and bathroom. The kitchen was through rather a grand archway as you came through the front door into the left of the square room downstairs.

Nick and I grew closer as the months passed and I found myself taking on more tasks involved with the day-to-day running of the pub, including dealing with accounts, ordering beers from the brewery and shopping with him for crisps, nuts and all the other bits and pieces necessary. Eventually it was decided I should move in. My landlord had reversed his decision and put the rent up to what it was previously when Katy had been living there with me. Above the pub were many rooms that were not used. It was in a dreadful state, Nick not being into housework at all. The kitchen had every appliance imaginable in it. There were two huge living rooms on the first floor, a sizeable bathroom and three bedrooms. On the floor above were three more bedrooms. He had two dogs living up there – a small Jack Russell called Toby and a huge German shepherd by the name of Shadow. The terrier frequently leapt on people passing by below the kitchen window if he knew them – not a mean feat as it was on the first floor, but he never injured himself.

All the customers put two and two together and came up with five, of course. We weren't actually having any sort of relationship then. Of course, working side by side behind the bar and spending all our spare time together inevitably led to more, and soon we were sharing our lives completely. If we ever wanted to have a break, we would jump in Nick's Land Rover and roar up over the moors. He let me drive occasionally, which was great fun; but I wasn't a very good driver, which I'm sure gave him a few grey hairs. On the occasions I managed to get away on my own I would take Shadow for long walks on a local beach which boasted three miles of golden sand. Shadow loved it and would run until he was exhausted. We would both come back exhilarated!

Nick and I sometimes had customers we knew well upstairs after hours, but we usually regretted it as at the end of the day we were both so tired and they often didn't want to leave. I invited my friends round too, of course, but Nick was very wary of them, knowing their habits and my previous ones.

Occasionally someone would pick a fight with Nick, but without much success. He was six feet four inches and usually came out of it without much difficulty. One night, however, I came across him in the corridor between the bar and lounge buried under a pile of bodies. I summoned the locals and the bodies were swiftly dealt with. Whoever started it came back that night and was climbing around on the roof screaming abuse and waving a knife. Eventually we grew tired of him and the police were called. He spent the night cooling off in a cell.

After months of constant harassment I decided I badly needed a break. The summer season was over and the pub had quietened down considerably. I knew if I told Nick, he wouldn't let me go easily, so I left him a note and crept away early one morning. I had more money than I could possibly need by this time, so caught a train and went to see my parents. I had been there exactly four hours when the phone rang and a hysterical Nick was at the other end. I was amazed. He had apparently misread my note, got it all hopelessly wrong, was madly in love with me and was on his way to London. He must have had his foot to the floor all the way as he arrived very quickly and ushered me into the Land Rover. I didn't say anything for a while as I felt very awkward. I certainly wasn't in love with him. He was kind and generous and I was very fond of him, but love? No.

He took me past Heathrow Airport and I idly remarked that I had never flown. Before I knew it we were in the airport terminal and he was asking for the first available flight anywhere. Fortunately it was a short haul to Dublin. Before long we were strapped in our seats, then tearing down the runway and up into the night. It was dark when we took off and, looking down at all the lights as we flew across the inky sky, England appeared to resemble fairyland to me.

The flight was a short one – about an hour, I think. At the airport we were whisked off to a hotel by taxi. I can't remember how long we stayed, but we had a fabulous time. We went to all the best restaurants and I was thoroughly spoilt. It was almost Christmas then, and he bought me clothes, books, jewellery (I had my ears pierced while I was there), perfume and masses of silk underwear. We didn't walk anywhere, always having a taxi to take us where we needed to go.

Nick had left Wendy in charge of the pub in our absence, and we had some reliable staff by then, so when we arrived home everything was running smoothly. The three of us spent Christmas together; he bought me yet another gift, which he presented to me on Christmas morning – a small cardboard box with holes punched in the lid. When I opened it there sat a tiny Siamese kitten. She was a beautiful cream with milk-chocolate colouring and blue eyes. I immediately named her Tai Lu. When I was a small child I was given a book called *Tai Lu Talking*, and from that I hankered after a life in Devon with a Siamese cat. So my wishes had come true! She would sit on the corner of the bar while I was working and the customers would feed her cheese-and-onion crisps, which she loved. I also discovered she had a passion for strawberry blancmange!

It was an enjoyable time, although I had an uncomfortable feeling this situation was not really what I was looking for now I found myself part of a couple. Nick was very loving and attentive almost to the point of suffocation. He was really rather possessive. He had some very strange habits in the bedroom, involving ropes and handcuffs and other more bizarre items, which quite frightened me; but on the whole he was the ideal partner. If only I felt the same way as he did! But although I was very fond of him he was rather straight-laced and tended towards criticism of my friends and lifestyle, at which I took umbrage.

It was hard work acting as landlady, but I enjoyed it. The pub had a quiz team and two darts teams. The ladies' darts team, which we named The Six Blind Mice, captained by me, were reasonably successful and gave us all the opportunity to visit other pubs in the area and meet the landladies and bar staff who worked in them; it also gave me some much needed time off. Nick and I could rarely be absent together, which suited me. I couldn't have coped being with him all the time anyway.

Katy by now had her baby, a beautiful chubby little boy. She called him Oliver and he was a miniature version of her. He had auburn hair, long, sweeping eyelashes and huge expressive eyes. I went to see her a couple of times. She was living in a semi in Bristol with the child's father, whom I didn't actually meet as when I visited he was usually working. She was absolutely besotted with that child, and it was lovely to see. She lived in a different world to me now, and although there was now coolness between us I understood and wished her well, knowing I quite probably would not be seeing her again. I was happy things had worked out so well for her, but rather sad that our days together drifting through life had come to an end. She was surprised I was now with Nick, but worried I was once again in a relationship that was wrong for me. I assured her that the thought of being with Nick on a permanent basis and having children scared me to death.

I was reasonably content at that time, though Nick was becoming very secretive. However, I was so busy I really didn't pay much attention. Wendy had by now moved into the pub with us and helped behind the bar, which left me free to deal with the mountain of paperwork that would somehow appear almost overnight. I still had my friends and on quiet evenings, of which there weren't many, they would sit at the bar and talk to me. The drugs took hold of quite a few and I lost two good friends through accidental overdoses.

Eventually I discovered that Nick and Wendy were having an affair. Nick was full of apologies, and although my pride was hurt I was actually quite relieved. I wanted to move out in a hurry, and I found yet another attic flat. It was tiny, but big enough for one. I stayed there for a week or so. Nick came to see me and wasn't impressed with the flat at all. He moved me to the house he had bought for his now ex-wife and gave me the German shepherd for company. Of course I took my Siamese cat as well. The house was a mid-terrace property in a quiet street behind the main shopping area of the town. On the ground floor was one room with a small kitchenette, a small shower cubicle and an outside toilet full of spiders. Upstairs there were two small bedrooms. I chose the front, as the rear bedroom ceiling had collapsed and was now on the floor. The whole house was in a state of chaos. Nick's wife had seemingly left in a great hurry and there were toys and clothes strewn everywhere. I put it all in bags and left it in the corner of one of the bedrooms for Nick to collect at a later date. The furniture was reasonable and Nick bought me a television, so I was comfortable enough.

My friends started to visit – just a trickle at first as they knew

Nick and Wendy and all felt rather awkward with the situation. When they realised how happy I was, however, they came in their droves and once again I took up the old life of parties and just having fun. Nick came around from time to time and hinted things were not going as well as he had hoped between him and Wendy. Now their relationship had been made public the excitement of secrecy had gone. He started to visit more and more, and it soon became clear he wanted a secret affair with me while still living with Wendy. No way!

The first thing I needed to do was get a job so I wouldn't have to rely on Nick for money. I then needed to move away from the house and find a flat. Back to the employment agency I went once again. I wanted a job in the nearest big town so I wouldn't keep bumping into Nick or Wendy. I soon found one as a bonus clerk in an engineering factory. It was only a bus ride away and I soon settled in. I had an office in the middle of the shop floor surrounded by men and machinery. It was very noisy with a constant smell of oil. The atmosphere there was very relaxed and friendly and I was treated as one of the boys.

One of the men there lived just around the corner from my house, so he offered me a lift there and back every day. I found this ideal as it was now autumn once again and winter would soon be upon us and I would not have to stand in the cold and rain waiting for buses and spend the day in damp clothing. We got to know each other quite well and I told him of my situation. He suggested I move into his girlfriend's house. For some time she had been looking for a tenant who would occasionally look after her children and dogs, clean, cook and really be a good companion. I promised to visit her that evening.

On arriving home, I cooked a meal, fed Shadow and Tai Lu then made my way up to the house. It had five storeys, including a basement in which his girlfriend, Sally, lived, and it was set back from the road with access from a winding gravel path through the trees. It was hidden completely from the road – quite a secret hideaway, in fact.

Sally was a very friendly lady, but, after speaking to her for some time, I thought she appeared to be rather lonely. Her boyfriend couldn't be with her as he was separated from his wife and she had told him in no uncertain terms he would not be permitted to see his children if he moved in with Sally. She really wanted a friend, but someone who could also step in and take care of things when she was away. She had a tropical-fish business and was forever rushing off to some airport or other to collect the latest assignment; hence she really needed someone she could rely on when she had to hurry off. She also bred chow chows, huge beautiful dogs with thick coats, tails that curve across their backs and blue tongues! She had three bitches and they took up a lot of space. I couldn't of course take my German shepherd there, so sadly had to return him to the pub, with a story of not wanting to leave him all day while I was working. I didn't want to tell Nick I was moving in case he made a fuss, and I didn't want him to know where I was for a while. Once I had gone it didn't matter so much.

A few nights later – or actually very early one morning – a crowd of my friends (all sworn to secrecy, of course) were to be found piling all my belongings into the back of a battered old van one of them owned. Then off we went. Most of them had to walk, but fortunately it wasn't very far and soon we were all assembled in front of my new home. We all grabbed armfuls and in we went. Sally had decided to give me the top floor. Everyone was puffing and panting by the time all my belongings were safely delivered, and they all left.

The flat reminded me slightly of the flat in London (it was off a tiny staircase leading from the fourth-floor landing), and I drew crumbs of comfort from it. The tenants who had rented it previously hadn't done much to it at all. Most of the wallpaper was peeling off and the paintwork was yellow. It was a typical attic. All the rooms had sloping ceilings. The next day I set to work, bought some paint and started to put my own stamp on it. There was no furniture in the living room, so I bought huge squashy cushions in reds, blues and yellows and I painted the walls and the ceiling a very bright lime green. It looked wonderful – not exactly easy on the eye, but pretty spectacular. There was one window, a circle of stained glass, and the sun shining through created beautiful patterns on the floor and around the room. The bedroom had a bed, cupboard and wardrobe and I painted the walls and ceiling of this room a pale lilac. The carpet was stained here and there, so I bought small rugs and scattered them around. The bathroom had recently been decorated white and navy, and I quite liked that so left it as it was. The kitchen was a bit of a mess, but as I didn't intend to do much cooking I just cleaned it and left that as it was too.

I spent a lot of time with Sally down in the basement. Her living room was amazing. It was always dark and gloomy as she never opened the curtains, which were thick and heavy and reached to the floor. Fish tanks two or three deep lined every wall, and with the pumps and heaters running constantly the whole room hummed. The kitchen was chaotic with every shelf and workspace covered completely. These were the only two rooms I ever spent any time in.

She had two children, but they were only there for the holidays as they were both at boarding school. They came home for Christmas and New Year, delightful little boys, full of fun, very well mannered and well behaved. Nick had found out by now where I was and kept ringing, but Sally wouldn't let him speak to me. He started then to come around, but didn't get past the front door as she was a big, powerful woman and wouldn't let him near me. I bred my lovely Siamese cat while I was living there and she duly gave birth to a litter of six beautiful kittens, in my bed! Sally's fish were also breeding well and two of the dogs became mothers with Sally and me acting as midwives, so the days and nights were quite busy. Her boyfriend's ex-wife relented at last and he was allowed to bring his two daughters to Sally's for weekends and the occasional weekday evening.

I didn't see the other tenants often. Most of them were unemployed, spent their time in the various pubs and were usually fairly inebriated. They used to shout and fight at all hours of the night and day, but I felt quite safe whether in Sally's with the dogs, who were quite aggressive towards people they didn't know or like, or up locked away in my attic. I was still spending time with my friends and most nights found it difficult to negotiate the path between the trees and would often fall into them. Sometimes I could struggle out of their grasp, but often I would wake underneath trees in the early hours of the morning covered in leaves and twigs.

One by one Sally evicted all the other tenants in the house and it became quiet and peaceful. She was very wary of letting the rooms again – some of them had been quite badly damaged. They decided to sell then and move away. The house was expensive to maintain and needed money spent on it to return it to its former glory, so she decided to downsize to a smaller property somewhere.

CHAPTER TEN

I was left homeless once more, but I found another flat quite quickly and the same friends helped me move my belongings down all the stairs into the same scruffy van, and off we went once again. The flat I had found was once again on the top floor, but there were only three storeys this time. It was a modern building with a well-fitted but small kitchen, quite a luxurious bathroom, a spacious lounge with a wide window seat overlooking the sea, and a double bedroom. All the rooms had recently been decorated in pale, neutral colours so there was nothing to be done but unpack my belongings and settle in once again. I had kept two of Tai Lu's kittens – two males whom I named To To and Tigger. My friends continued to visit. The parties seemed almost continuous and I had a home once again.

I was still reasonably happy with my office job, but the travelling would become more difficult now I would not be having a lift any more. Winter dragged on with little sign of spring, so I was half-heartedly looking for something else. I had started to use another pub very close to my new home; it had a slightly different balance of clientele, and there was rarely any trouble.

I was talking with the landlord and his wife one evening, and of course they knew I had been running the pub up the road. They were looking for part-time staff and they asked me if I wanted the job. I had actually quite missed working behind a bar, so gave my notice in at the factory and was once again a barmaid. It was completely different from my previous employment. Everyone was very polite and well behaved. It was early in the season and was reasonably quiet, so I had plenty of time to acquaint myself with the layout of the bars, prices and so on. Unfortunately I was not earning enough to pay my rent, so looked around for another part-time post.

A job as a waitress in a bistro owned by friends of Nick became available. They were good to me and I had as much coffee as I wanted and a meal thrown in. And occasionally I found myself lending a hand in the kitchen, making hot drinks, washing up and generally helping out. I was only there for a few weeks, but when the landlord of the pub said he needed me on a full-time basis and I would have to leave the bistro they gave me a beautiful book full of soup recipes. I was very touched! I still have it, rather dog-eared and scruffy now, but written inside the first page was an inscription: 'to our friend Jen with best love, summer '75'.

Gradually the holidaymakers arrived and the pub became busy. The bar was very long, divided by a wall. The lounge bar was one end, a comfortable room with plush rose-pink seating and curtains; a deep-pile carpet covered the floor and the tables were highly polished dark wood with matching ladder-back chairs. The public bar was at the other end, with a flagstone floor and simple benches around the walls. I usually served in the bar unless I was needed to serve drinks in the lounge while the landlord went to the kitchen to collect the meals the customers had ordered. We had locals there too, but they were mostly young seasonal workers from the hotels. They were a lot of fun and treated me like a big sister. Sometimes at closing time a crowd would wait for me and take me on to a party or a club. There was an excellent jukebox in the bar, and it was playing constantly and very loudly. If I ever hear any songs by Barry White, I can shut my eyes and imagine myself back there.

The pub served excellent food and the landlady would do all the cooking. There was no cellar and the beer barrels were behind a wall running the length of the bar. The local fishermen brought crabs in cardboard boxes, which would be kept by the barrels, and they were always escaping and crawling around.

We were all very wary as we didn't want to get our toes pinched. I usually used to wear jeans and a thin vest with flip-flops on my feet. By the end of the night the area behind the bar would be awash with beer and we would all be paddling around trying to avoid the crabs! The landlord and landlady were really easy-going, and as long as we worked hard we could drink and chat – do what we liked really.

At closing time there was always a meal ready for me if I wanted it – usually something in a basket, but very welcome all the same. I don't recall ever buying groceries of any sort, although I must have. In fact, I don't remember very much at all about the whole of 1975 – just little snapshots, in no particular order, of people and places, snatches of music and conversation.

I was still there when Christmas came around, and of course I was asked to work. The pub was only open at lunchtime and, when we closed, tables were set out in the lounge with crisp white cloths, glasses and cutlery. We sat down to a delicious Christmas lunch – turkey and all the trimmings followed by pudding and cream. We then sat around talking and drinking until early evening before we all departed for home. I was so tired that I just crawled into bed and slept until the next day.

The pub was quiet now, but a decision was made to keep me on in a full-time post so my boss and his wife could spend more time together with their children and dogs. They had a son who was eleven years old, a daughter of eight and two dogs – a St Bernard and the smallest poodle I have ever seen. This tiny dog was definitely the boss. All very amusing! Meals were only offered in the evening, so only the two bars needed to be taken care of. Not many customers used the lounge – just the occasional tourist muffled up against the cold would sit and read the papers and nurse a drink for an hour or two. Most of our customers then were local tradesmen. Fishermen came in too. They were generous and brought me some of their catch from time to time. I'd go home to cook and clean what was on offer, then the cats and I would sit down to a feast. I occasionally fished myself, but it was easier and less time-consuming to accept the generosity of the locals.

Time passed quickly and summer came around again; the pub became busier once more. Meals were an all-day event and most of the hotel staff that had been with us the year before returned to take up their various posts, together with some new faces.

The town held a carnival every summer and in 1976 it was decided that we would have a float and take part. A lorry was borrowed and quite a few of the boys who used to frequent the bar collected twigs, ferns and straw. We obtained some lengths of green material and a short (very short!) tunic was fashioned for me to wear. The boys, who had decided they would ride on the float, all found (and dyed) jeans and T-shirts and found various headgear, which they decorated with feathers. I made a tall, pointed witch's hat, painted it green and stuck a length of cream voile to the top. The lorry was decorated to resemble a wood, the boys were equipped with bows and arrows, and the landlord supplied a barrel of lager. Then on the day of the carnival we all climbed into the undergrowth and we were off!

What fun it was! There were so many people all cheering and waving, throwing money into the buckets we had tied around the sides. We rumbled along, but unfortunately when we reached the end of the route two things happened: one of the Merry Men (by now the *Very* Merry Men) discovered the barrel of lager was already empty, and Maid Marion (me) fell off! After the boys had finished laughing they jumped down, picked me up and rolled me back on. The rest of the day passed in a haze, but I know we spent the night back in the pub still dressed for the parts we had played, with me serving behind the bar.

A barmaid's life was a strange existence. I would sleep well into the day and I was at my most active when most folks are winding down ready for bed. I remember the summer of 1976 so clearly. It was so hot – endless days of heat and sunshine. Customers were usually five or six deep at the bar, demanding cold cider, beers and lager in a vain attempt to cool off. Days between shifts were spent lazing on the beach until the heat drove me to walk on the cliffs to catch what little breeze was on offer. Nights would be spent holding late barbeques in coves not frequented by the droves of holidaymakers who seemed to arrive every day to enjoy that wonderful summer.

The weeks drifted by, and suddenly it was September, and the pub quietened down, the visitors left.

It was a special time of year when the yachting crowd would arrive, tumbling through the door all brown-skinned and so alive. They ate many meals with us and stayed after hours, and we all became firm friends. They were all Welsh with wonderful sing-song voices I adored instantly. There were many yachts moored in the harbour. They would all sail over together for long weekends and spend most of their time with us. It was during one of these drunken sessions, from which I was rarely excluded, that a dare was dangled before me like a carrot in front of a donkey: to rendezvous with the yacht, the *Gold Star*, a beautiful twenty-four-foot ocean-going vessel, a week thence, at a small French fishing village and sail her home. A member of the crew on the outward journey was apparently transferring to another boat, so they had room for another person on board. It took me about two minutes to decide I would go. The landlord, my boss, a huge, hairy, jolly man, thought I had gone completely crazy and the crew accepted my enthusiasm for a drunken woman's ramblings. All too soon they were spilling out into the street shouting their farewells and it was time to clear up, wash the glasses and make my way home to my flat.

The next day I tackled my boss and the time off was agreed upon. It was pretty quiet by then anyway. The summer was drawing to a close and most of the holidaymakers had left. I had been working long hours all the summer, often at short notice, and, as I was one of the best barmaids he had ever had, he thought I deserved a break. He was, however, concerned for my safety and doubted my ability to find my destination without getting completely lost.

The customers soon found out what I was up to and arranged a party for me. It was to be held in a club we used to frequent at the top of the cliffs in an old manor house. It opened its doors at midnight and closed around dawn. It was a dark, gloomy place with a dance floor no bigger than a handkerchief and dark corners with old sofas here and there where we could smoke anything we liked without disturbance. A small bar was to one side. Most of my friends were there, including George, who proceeded to become very drunk and begged me not to go.

We had an enjoyable night, but, looking around at them all, I realised suddenly none of them were really friends at all any more. They were all very heavy drinkers and drug users, and the majority of them now seemed to have lost their grasp on reality. I was becoming afraid now for my own sanity after all the stuff I had either smoked or swallowed over the years. The idea of an escape was immediately very appealing, and I hoped the time away would give me some space to re-evaluate my life and decided what I was to do next.

CHAPTER ELEVEN

I packed for the trip carefully, taking only a rucksack containing essential clothing, passport and a map, with what money I had tucked safely away, and my sleeping bag strapped securely on top. My moods swayed from excitement to panic and then slight hysteria. I ate what little food was left in the kitchen and took the cats to my friend's house, where I knew they would be well looked after, then set off.

The first part of the journey was uneventful. I had good lifts all the way to Dover, reaching the ferry terminal in ample time to catch the next sailing. I was now very nervous. I have always had a fear of large ships, and I cannot even speak about the liner that tragically sank in April 1912 or look at a picture of her in a book without a feeling of complete terror. I tried to put my fears aside, and although I was trembling I marched on to the ferry and found a corner, shook out my sleeping bag and, using my rucksack as a pillow, lay down.

Soon the engines were throbbing beneath me and then I felt a sense of movement and I knew there was no turning back. I began to think of the journey ahead and knew I had quite an adventure in front of me as we sailed away from England and the White Cliffs vanished from view. The sea was very rough. Most of the passengers around me periodically lurched off, no doubt to part with the meal they had unfortunately just eaten. I admit to feeling a little queasy, but whether that was due to the pitching and heaving of the vessel or the state of my nerves I couldn't say. I had tossed and turned most of the previous night, but now I was soon asleep.

I woke with a start and felt no movement nor the sound of the engines, so scrambled up, gathered my belongings and found the ladies' toilet. There I washed my hands and face and generally tidied myself up. I then joined the queue, longing for firm soil beneath my feet, offering up a silent prayer for my safety.

Fortunately the weather was in my favour and, armed with my map, I set off from the dockside. It was far easier than I imagined. A vehicle soon stopped for me and I merely pointed to the map, smiled and hopped in. The driver and I communicated mostly by mime as I couldn't speak any French at all. After he set me down and pointed in the direction I needed to go I shook his hand and watched him disappear into the distance. The second and third lifts were equally pleasant, and the fourth driver spoke good English. The fifth, however, wasn't so good and I had to resort to my trusty pepper pot and hatpin. I had carried them with me since my schooldays and they had served me well. I decided to walk the rest of the way. It was only around two miles, but time was passing swiftly and I was eager to catch the *Gold Star* before she left without me. She couldn't wait as I knew she would have to leave on the next tide.

I reached the little town eventually and found the marina with ease. There were many craft there of all shapes and sizes. I ran around in despair until suddenly I heard a Welsh voice. There she was – the *Gold Star*! I slowed to a stroll and, when I reached her, leant over and knocked on the side of the boat, asking if they had a vacancy for crew, and if so could I please sign on for their next trip, which I knew was to Devon. The crew all went absolutely wild when they realised who it was, and I was carried on board. Everyone was talking at once, but eventually they all calmed down and I had the opportunity to study the faces around me.

The first was Desmond. He was the skipper and the owner of the *Gold Star*. He was, and probably still is, the richest man I have ever known. As well as that wonderful yacht, he had homes dotted around the continent and Great Britain. He also owned a string of shops and a couple of restaurants. He was a tall, gentle man with a deep, rich voice, smiling grey eyes, not a lot of hair and a huge beak of a nose. He was not unattractive, however; he was warm and funny with a great dry humour, probably in his mid forties.

Next to him was Belinda. She was tiny with short curly hair curling round her delicate features. She wore tortoiseshell glasses, behind which her eyes were bright and dark. Her smile was friendly enough, but from the possessive way she was holding Desmond's arm and gazing up at him it was obvious to me they were a couple and I felt she could become very unpleasant if another woman came along to steal her claim.

Next was Stuart – big blue eyes and lots of curly, longish fair hair. He was broad-shouldered and narrow-hipped, probably just under six feet tall.

Carl was also a big man, but very dark with swept-back hair, big, bushy eyebrows and a long, straight nose. His eyes seemed almost black and he smiled at me shyly. He would prove to be the quietest on board.

Alex was what I could only describe as a pretty boy. He wasn't much taller than Belinda and certainly shorter than me at five feet four. He had cropped brown hair and a baby face with mournful brown eyes. He was very slim with tiny wrists, long fingers and fine features. He and Carl were inseparable.

There were two couples, which meant Stuart and I would be together on watch, sleeping and looking after the general running of the boat. I wasn't complaining. They were all dressed in a similar fashion – shorts and casual shirts with deck shoes on their feet.

I was shown around. The *Gold Star* was compact and well designed. The forward cabin was surprisingly large and continued into the bow. There were bunks on either side with sloping sides, which I discovered later were essential at sea. Further back and to one side was a shower and toilet, and opposite was the galley, which is apparently the nautical term for a kitchen. At the stern of the boat was the master cabin, which mostly comprised a double bed. In the centre were two seats built up high for good all-round visibility and, of course, the huge wooden wheel to steer her by. It was all very pleasing. I was shown where to stow my belongings and where, when not on watch, I would sleep.

After a shower and a change of clothes it was decided that they would sail round the coast on the tide to a bay they knew well and were fond of and have a good meal before anchoring for the night and setting sail for home the next day. I watched as the crew started a routine I learned to love. They all knew exactly what to do, and soon we were motoring gently away from our berth and out into the open sea. Once again the crew danced about, and soon the sails were up, flapping in the breeze. The engine was then cut and the only sound accompanying the moving sails was the slap of the ocean as we cut through the water. As I was the only crew member with no immediate role to play I was sent to the stern with an attached safety wire complete with a bucket, hook and line to catch the following day's breakfast. It was an exhilarating experience, perched there with the wind in my hair and the sun on my face, the sound of the hull slicing through the calm blue water and the sails rippling in the breeze. I soon had a bite and caught six fish in total. I learnt then one of the rules on board: if one caught a fish, a shot of neat whisky had to be drunk in one gulp. I was eventually hauled back to the cabin, and with all the alcohol inside me I was feeling warm and happy.

Soon we were dropping anchor in a tiny, secluded, picturesque bay, and to my horror found we had to climb down into a small dinghy and row ashore. Desmond took Carl, Alex and me first. How I managed to negotiate those slippery steps and reach the swaying dingy without receiving a thorough dunking I will never know! Perhaps it was all that alcohol in my veins keeping me so relaxed. I soon found myself on dry land while Desmond rowed smoothly away to collect Stuart and Belinda.

The restaurant was all I imagined it to be – so utterly French and absolutely charming. It was a warm, sultry evening, so it was decided that we would dine outside in the courtyard.

Desmond ordered for me as the menu was in French, and we sat back talking quietly until our meal arrived. We began with an enormous salad topped with crisp green leaves and plump ripe tomatoes all drizzled with delicious olive oil. I fell upon it hungrily. With all the fresh air and whisky I was ravenous. The salad disappeared and I sat back in anticipation, waiting for the next course to arrive. The waiter appeared with a gigantic silver tray, and upon it lay a whole spider crab. I was speechless. There were tools provided, but Stuart could see I was rather mystified. He, of course, had seen it all before, and after much cracking and prodding it was ready to eat. It was delicious, if rather messy. There were sticks of French bread warm from the oven, pats of golden butter and, to follow, tasty wedges of cheese. Bottle after bottle of wine appeared. It was a feast for a king.

Soon it was dusk and the warmth of the sun was gone. Reluctantly we left the restaurant and made our way back to the dinghy. Desmond poured me in and rowed back to the yacht in the twilight with stars beginning to pepper the sky and the oars rhythmically slapping the water. Full of food and fine wine, I felt utter contentment.

I don't recall much after that, and woke the next morning fully clothed in my bunk with a sore head and dry mouth. I wasn't allowed to linger for long. I had to cook breakfast. The fish had been gutted and cleaned the evening before. I cooked them under the swaying grill with just fresh herbs and black pepper. We had brought some of the French sticks back with us from the restaurant and were soon gathered together forking down the fish and munching on the French bread. We followed with fruit and coffee.

Desmond was keen to set off, so Stuart and I cleared up while the remainder of the crew made ready. It was imperative we were properly dressed for the journey and wore our yellow life jackets and waterproofs at all times when on deck. I stayed in the cabin while Desmond shouted instructions; the anchor was hauled up and we were off. Some distance from the shoreline the sails were raised, and they quickly filled in the wind. The engines were cut and we were soon making good progress as the yacht sliced proudly through the water. Only parts of the voyage clearly stay in my memory. At some point the sails were taken down and the engines were chugging underneath us once more. Time meant nothing – just sharp images of huge seas and the waves like rolling hills. We climbed then fell, to rise on the next wave. We seemed so small in that great expanse of ocean with just the sea on either side, behind and before us and endless sky. I was assured that the weather was set fair, calm with light winds. The *Gold Star* was on autopilot by this time and we took turns, in pairs, to keep watch. All on deck as we crossed the shipping lanes, we were well aware that the tankers crossing first in front then behind us were huge beasts and took a long time to manoeuvre or stop, so we kept at a safe distance. Attached firmly by safety lines we perched on our high seats.

I remember taking one of the night watches with Stuart, who was very knowledgeable and an experienced sailor. I was shown how to recognise other craft in the darkness by their lights – green for starboard and red for port. Also, to my amazement, I learnt that lighthouses can be recognised by the pulse of their beam. At the end of that night watch I carefully slid into my bunk, grateful for the sloping sides, or I would have been tipped out again and again as she rolled, swayed and shuddered.

I must have slept because Stuart was suddenly by my side shaking me gently and whispering that we were on watch again. I dressed quickly, pulled on waterproofs and donned my life jacket. Andy and Carl, who were on watch before us, smiled a greeting then melted away as Stuart and I took their place on the lurching deck. Although we were on autopilot, things could go disastrously wrong, so we reported all we saw, felt and heard before handing over to the next pair. It was very quiet as we sat together with the water sparkling beneath us and the salty spray on our faces. Apart from a distant trawler we saw little, and as the dawn crept across the sky I felt such peace I almost wished that voyage could go on for ever.

Our watch soon came to an end and Desmond appeared, rubbing sleep from his eyes, stretching and yawning. Stuart and

I returned to the cabin, where Carl and Alex were gently snoring. We snuggled into our bunks once again and were soon sleeping.

I woke sometime later to hear Desmond's voice shouting for refreshment and was soon back in the galley grilling smoky bacon and making fresh, strong coffee for us all.

Soon we saw land in the distance, which was at first just a faint shadow on the horizon. Desmond told me then that they were unable to take me back as a miscalculation meant we had missed the tide and there would not have been enough water to take us safely into harbour. So we continued to Wales, where Belinda said I could stay with her for a few days until arrangements were made to take me back by road to Devon.

We anchored safely and said our goodbyes. It was with some considerable sadness I left the *Gold Star* which had been my temporary home, and I felt tears pricking my eyes as I walked away. Belinda took me under her wing, and we were soon travelling through narrow streets with strange names. Her flat was in a block set in pretty landscaped gardens. It was rather grand with large, spacious rooms and heating underfoot. She installed me in the guest room, which was homely and comfortable.

In the following days, while Belinda was working, I had time to think about my future. I realised I had become disenchanted with my life in Devon and that it had become false and shallow. I had become very aware of the loss of my friends through their drug habits and realised then that if I stayed maybe that's all life would hold for me – endless parties with drink, drugs and loneliness. I wanted something new, something different, something satisfying. I had never even visited Wales before, and from what I heard and saw over the following weeks it seemed a friendly place. Perhaps I could make my home here? I promised myself six months, after which I would return to Devon if I was not satisfied with my life.

Belinda took me back home the following weekend, and while she went to do some shopping I visited the friends who had taken care of the cats while I had been away. I explained the situation and they agreed to care for To To and Tigger until my return, or on a permanent basis if I decided to stay in Wales. I would of course take Tai Lu with me. I went back to pack what I could, then set off to see the landlord of the flat, who was the owner of the hotel where I'd had my first job.

The journey back to Wales was extremely harrowing with a very angry Siamese cat howling in her basket all the way there. She settled quickly, however, once we arrived back at Belinda's flat, and the next day I went, by train, to the town where most of the crew lived. It was a pleasure to see them all again. We had a meal together then went to Steve's flat, where I spent the night before I headed off in search of work. I managed to secure a job with the local council as a bonus clerk after having an interview in a local pub. I found a flat close by with ease as my future boss seemed to know everyone in the pub and soon found someone who had an empty property. The flat was opposite a very good chip shop, so I knew I wouldn't go hungry. Belinda kindly moved my belongings and I settled in.

I began work the following Monday, 8 November, and at eleven o'clock in the morning of that day I met the lovely man I am married to now, although I married, divorced and had two children in between.

There is a song in my mind now – something along the lines of 'Life happens when you are busy making other plans.' How very true! If I had not sailed across the sea in response to a drunken dare in that beautiful yacht, and had Desmond not miscalculated and missed the tide that would have carried me home, where would I be now?